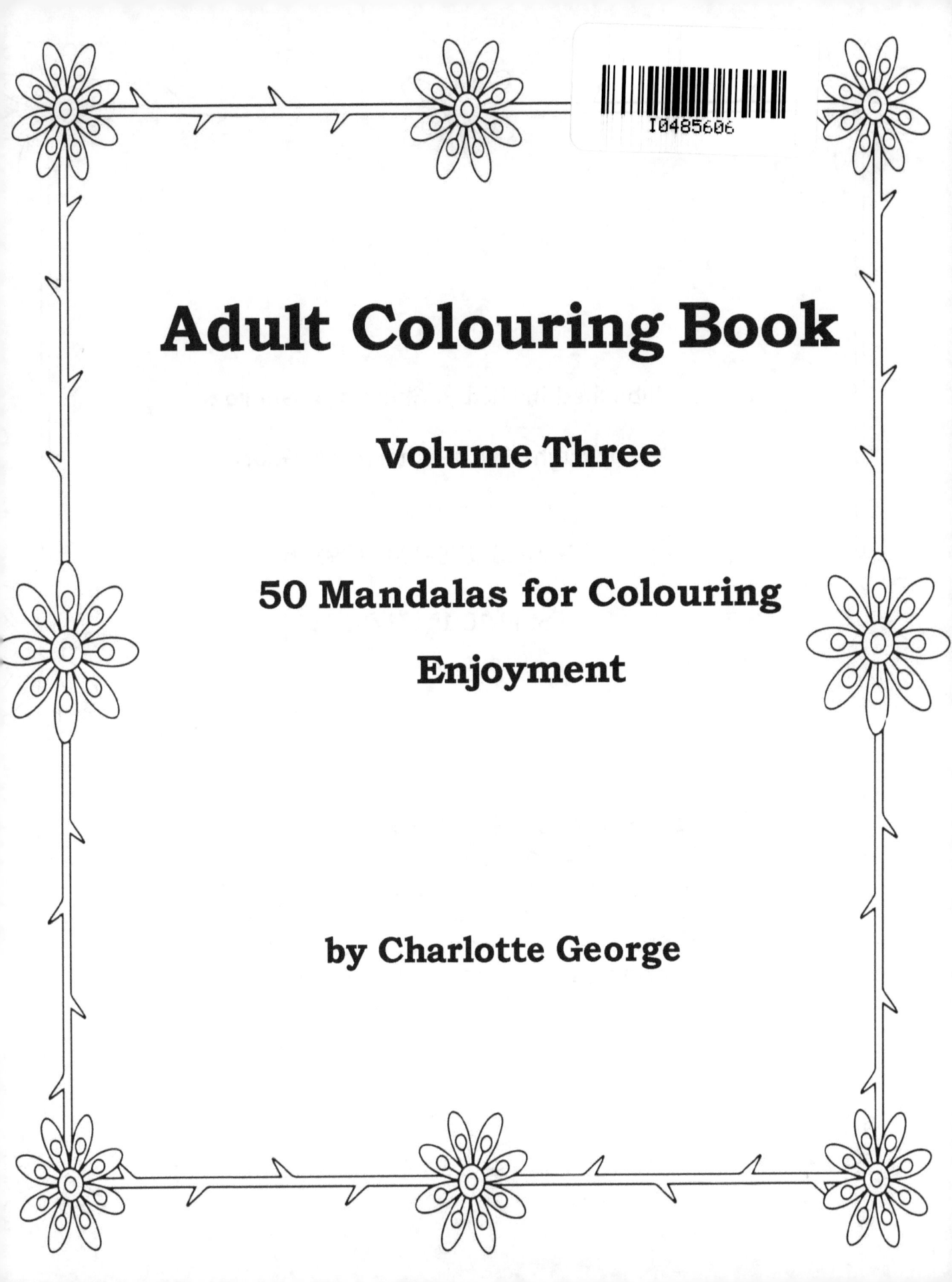

Adult Colouring Book

Volume Three

50 Mandalas for Colouring

Enjoyment

by Charlotte George

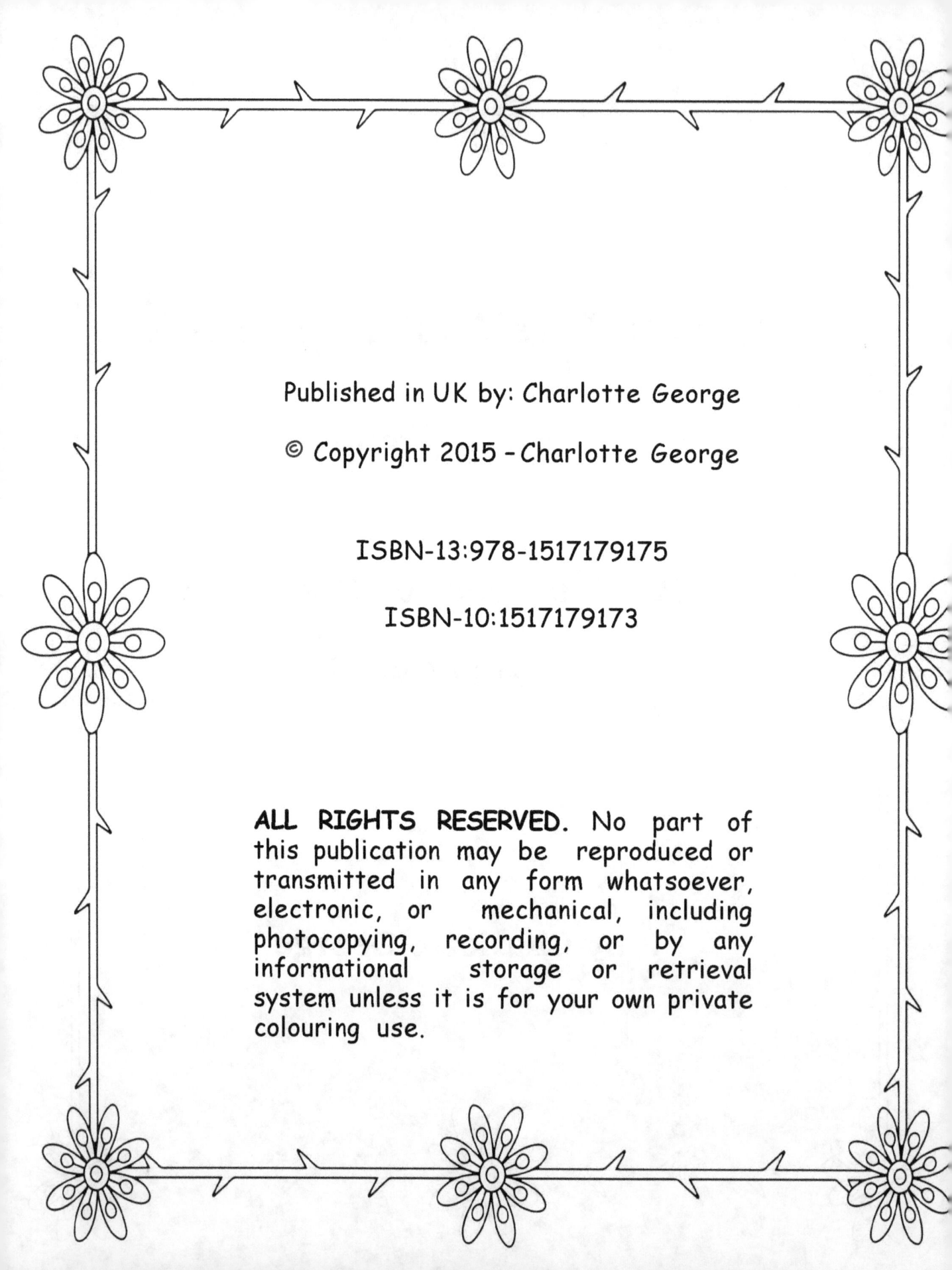

Published in UK by: Charlotte George

© Copyright 2015 – Charlotte George

ISBN-13:978-1517179175

ISBN-10:1517179173

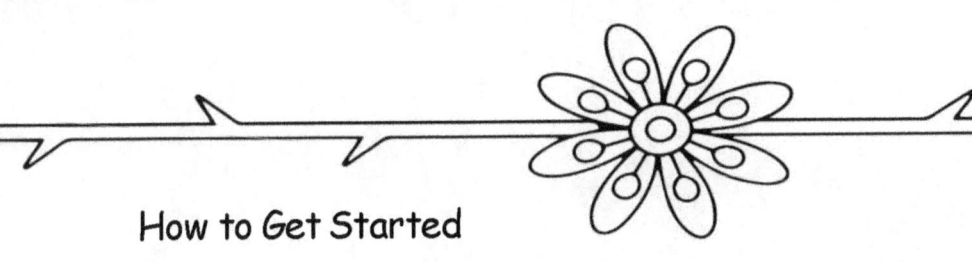

How to Get Started

This is Volume Three of my Mandalas colouring series and I hope you get as much enjoyment out of this one as you have from the previous volumes.

There are some easy and quick ones to get your imagination going as well as some really detailed ones that will take a little longer. You choose according to your mood.

Follow this simple process to gain the most from colouring this book.

- Find somewhere quiet and relaxing to do your colouring and make sure you are set up comfortably on a flat surface if possible.

- Switch off your phone, tablet, computer or other media.

- Turn to a page in the book that you can relate to or really like and begin colouring. Enjoy the pleasure of drifting into a stress free state of mind and forget all the everyday worries.

You will be surprised how quickly colouring becomes addictive and how much enjoyment you get from something this simple.

Allow yourself to have hours of stress free enjoyment as well as becoming mentally relaxed without even trying.

So what are you waiting for, pick up your pens and just start colouring.

Happy Colouring
Charlotte

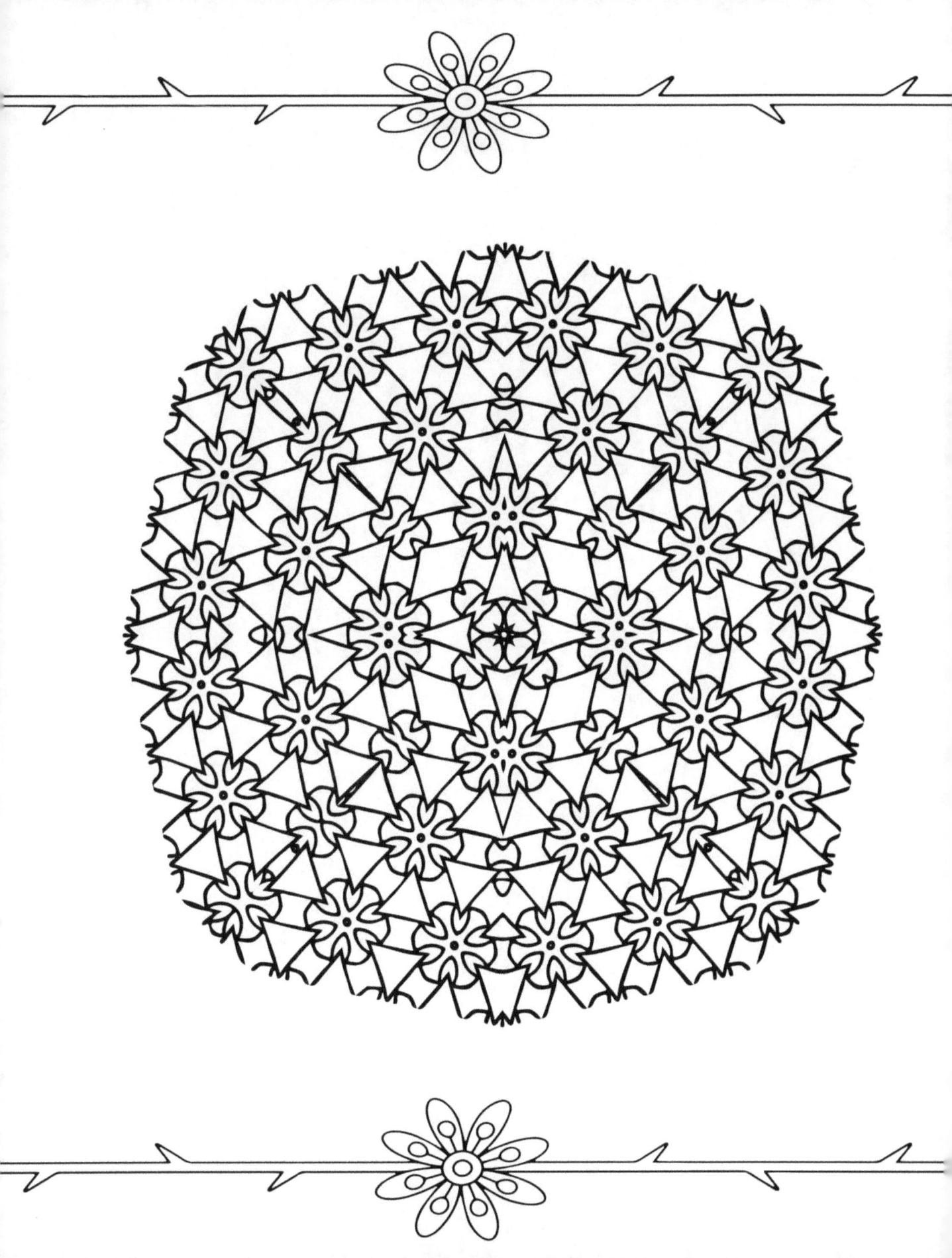

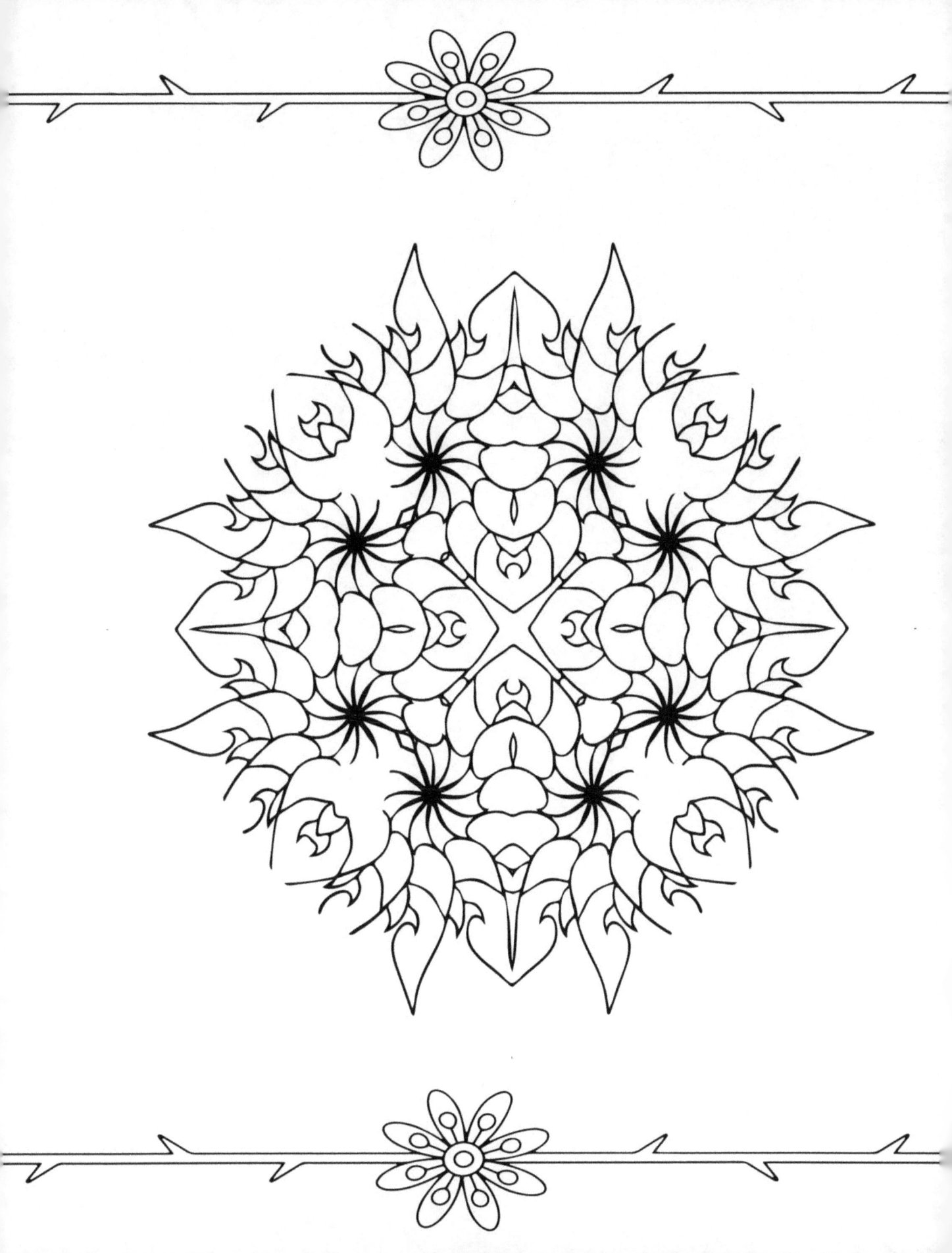

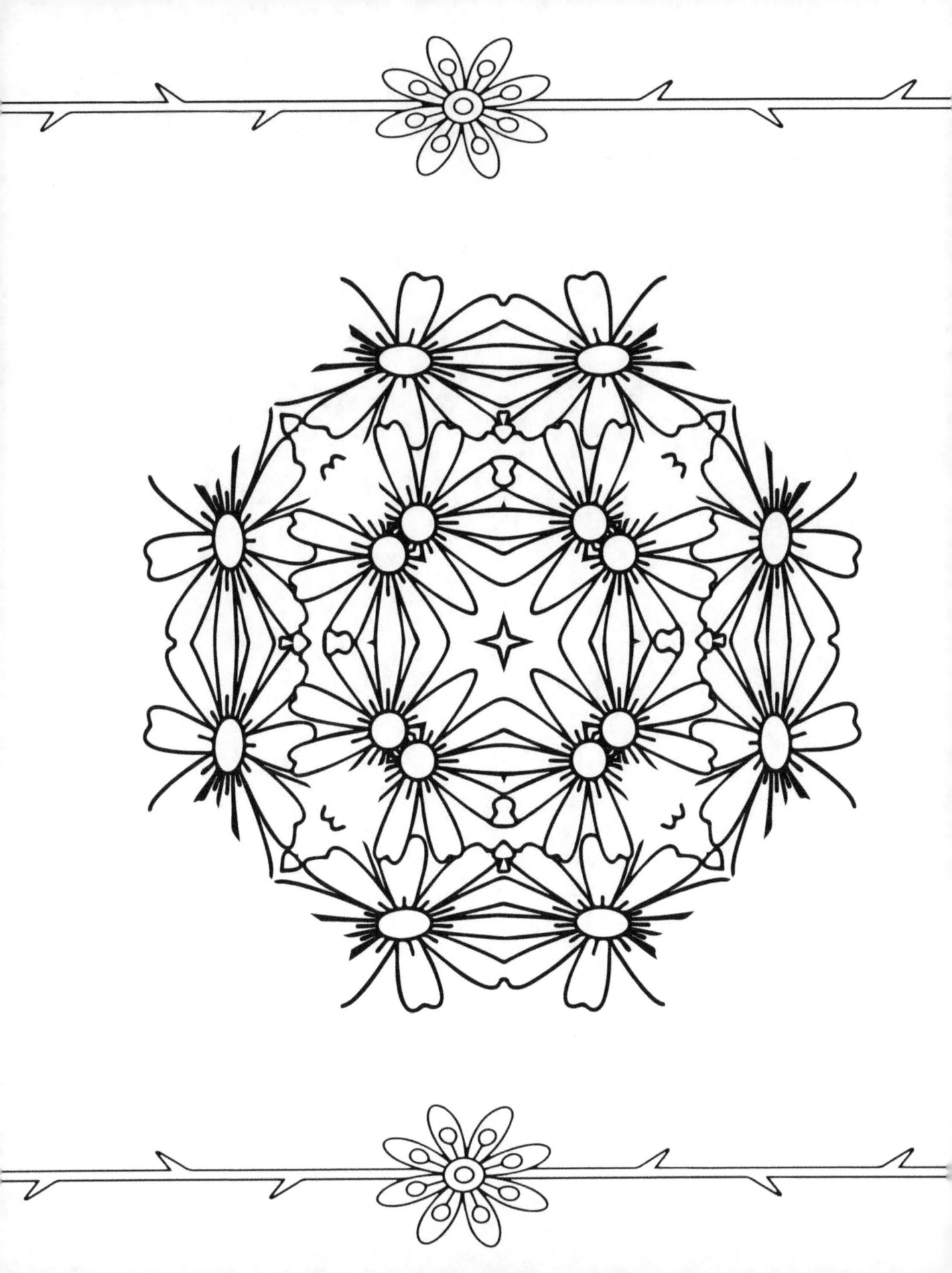

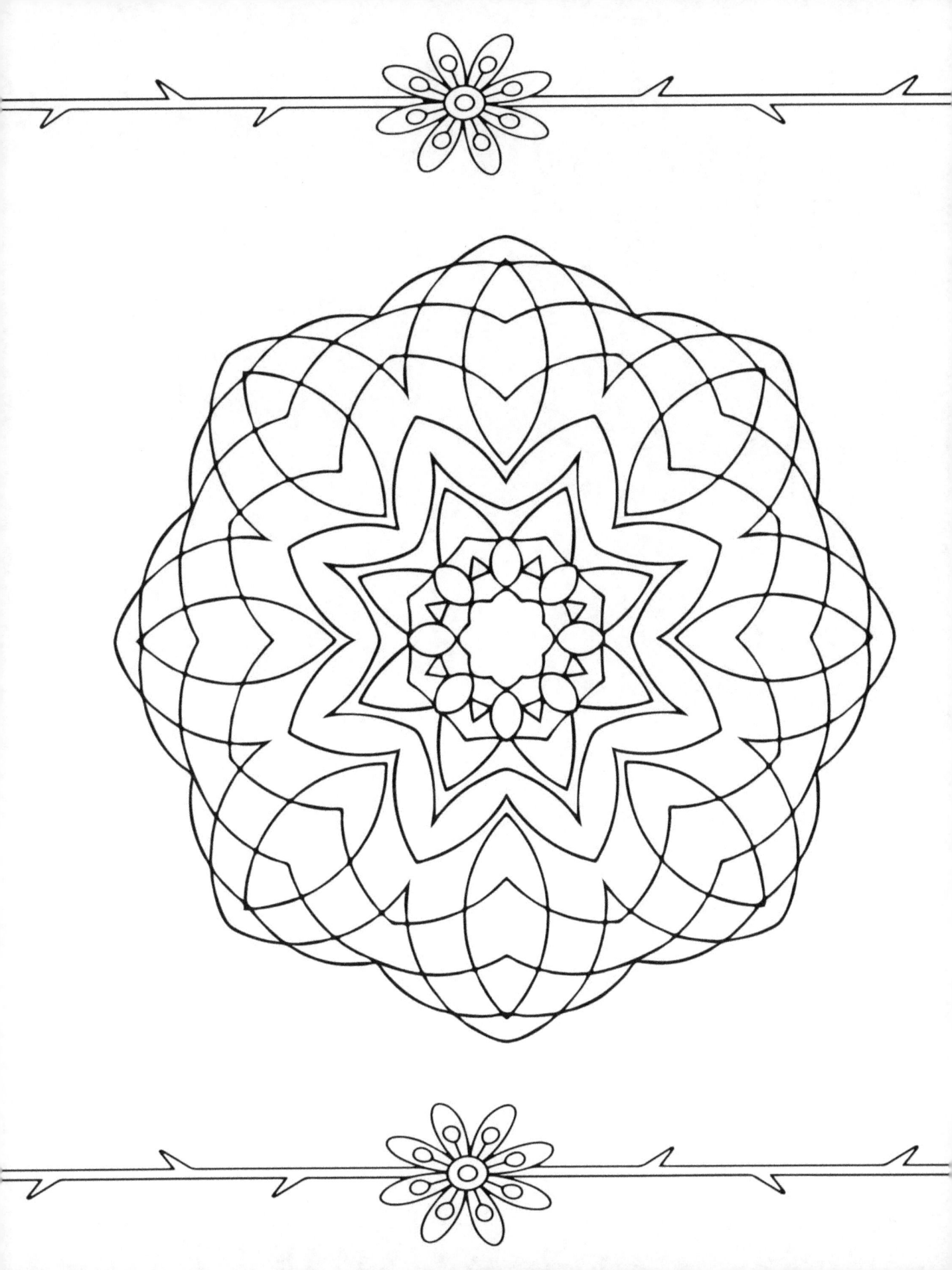

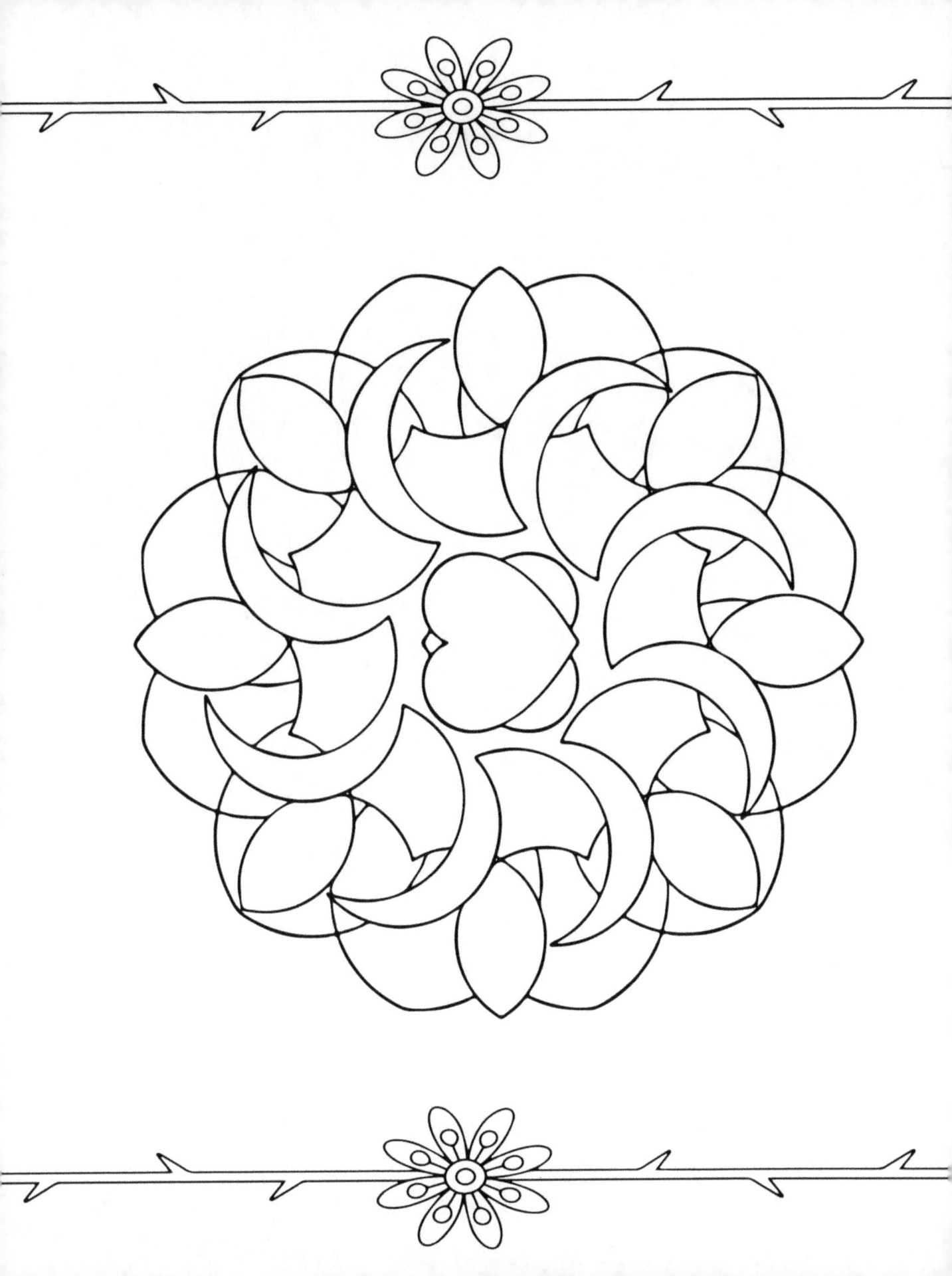

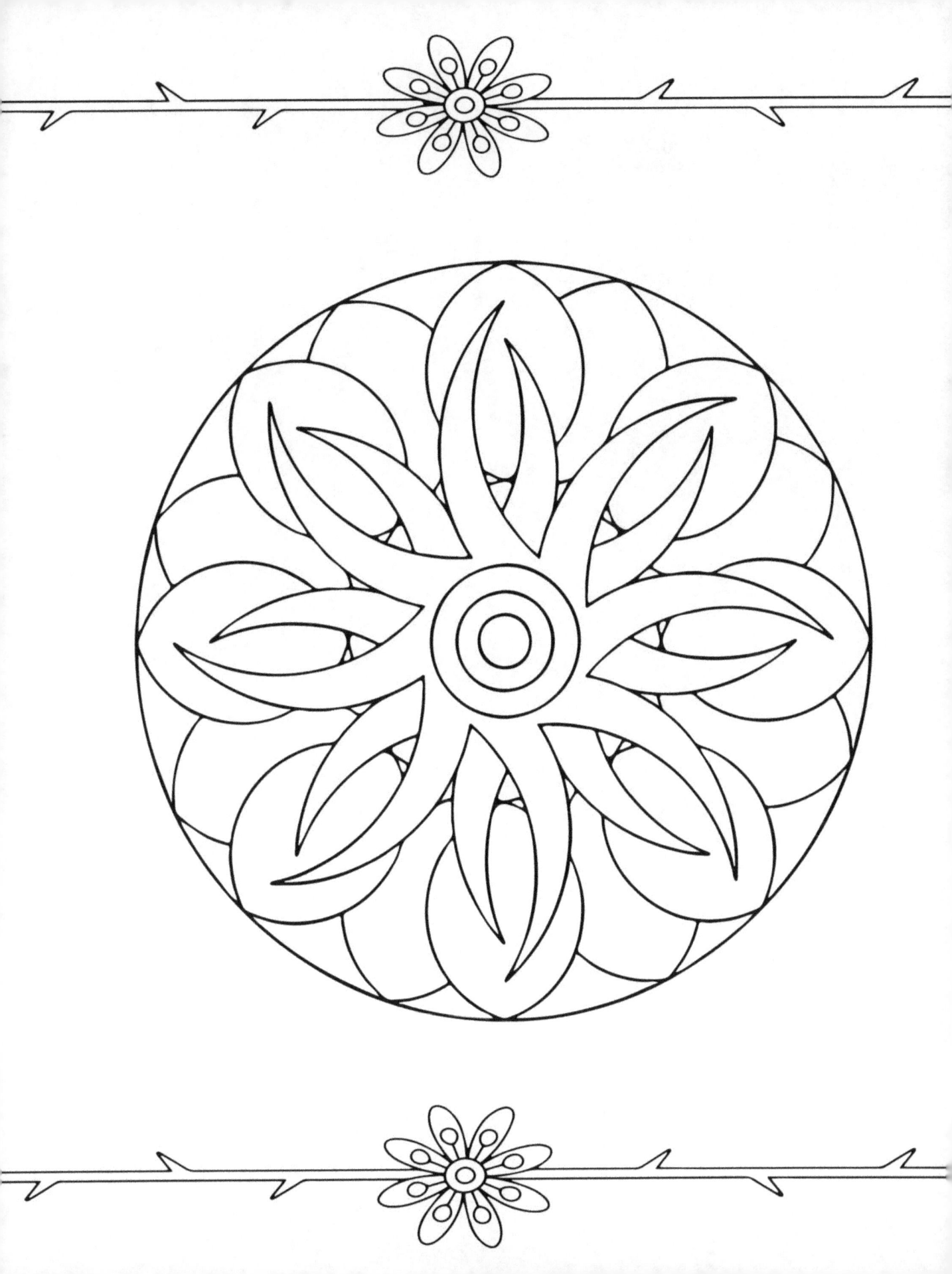

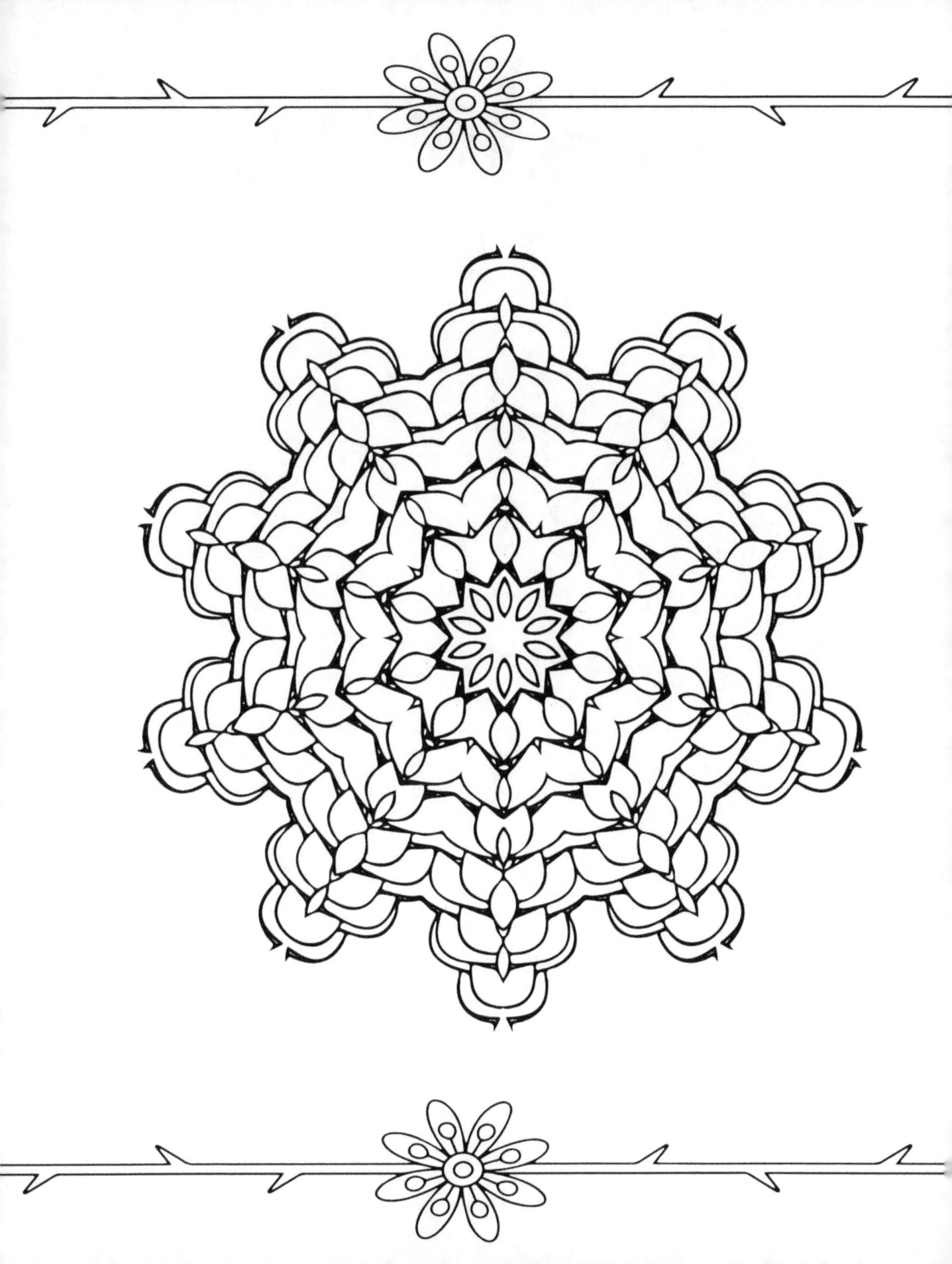

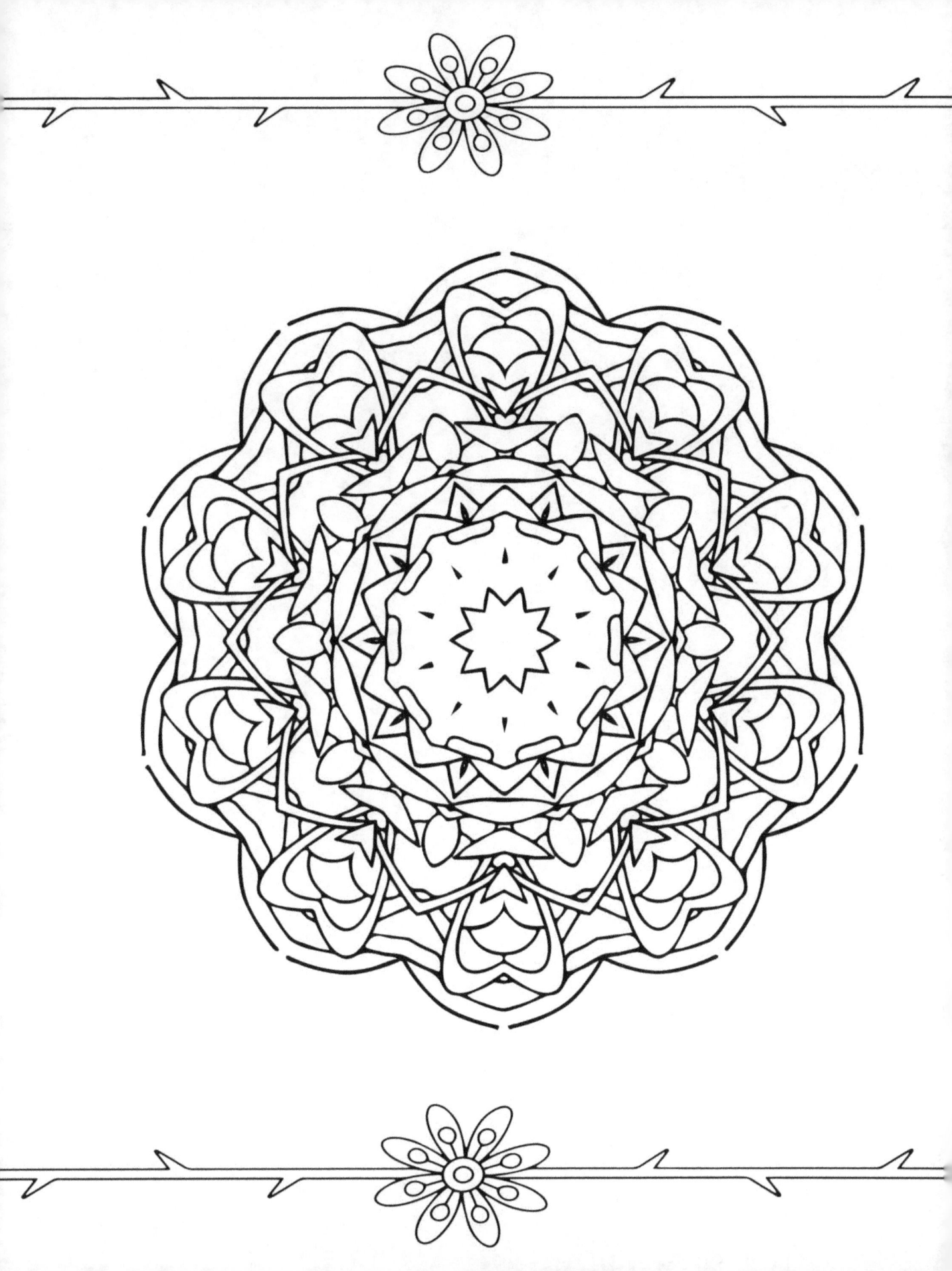

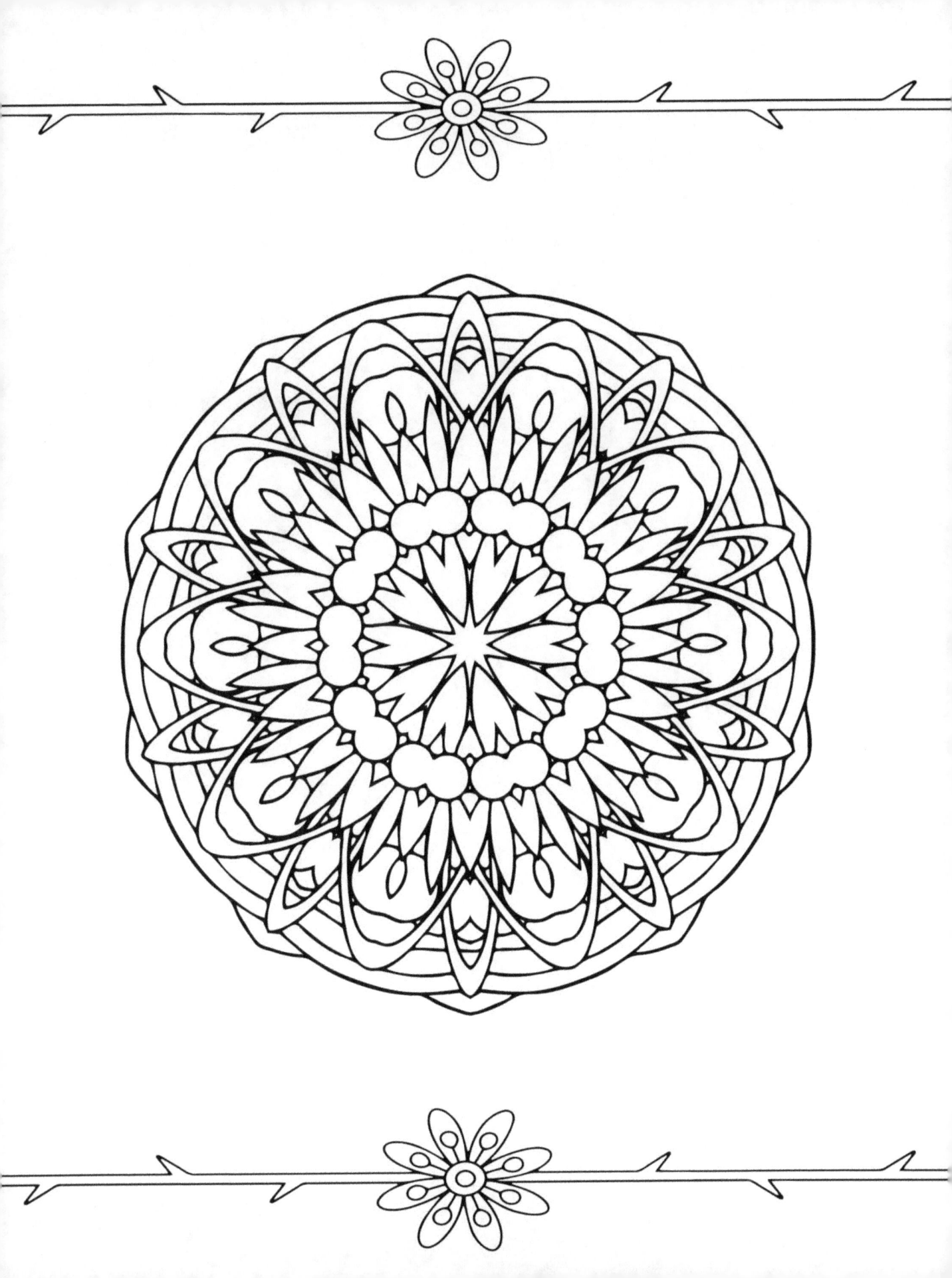

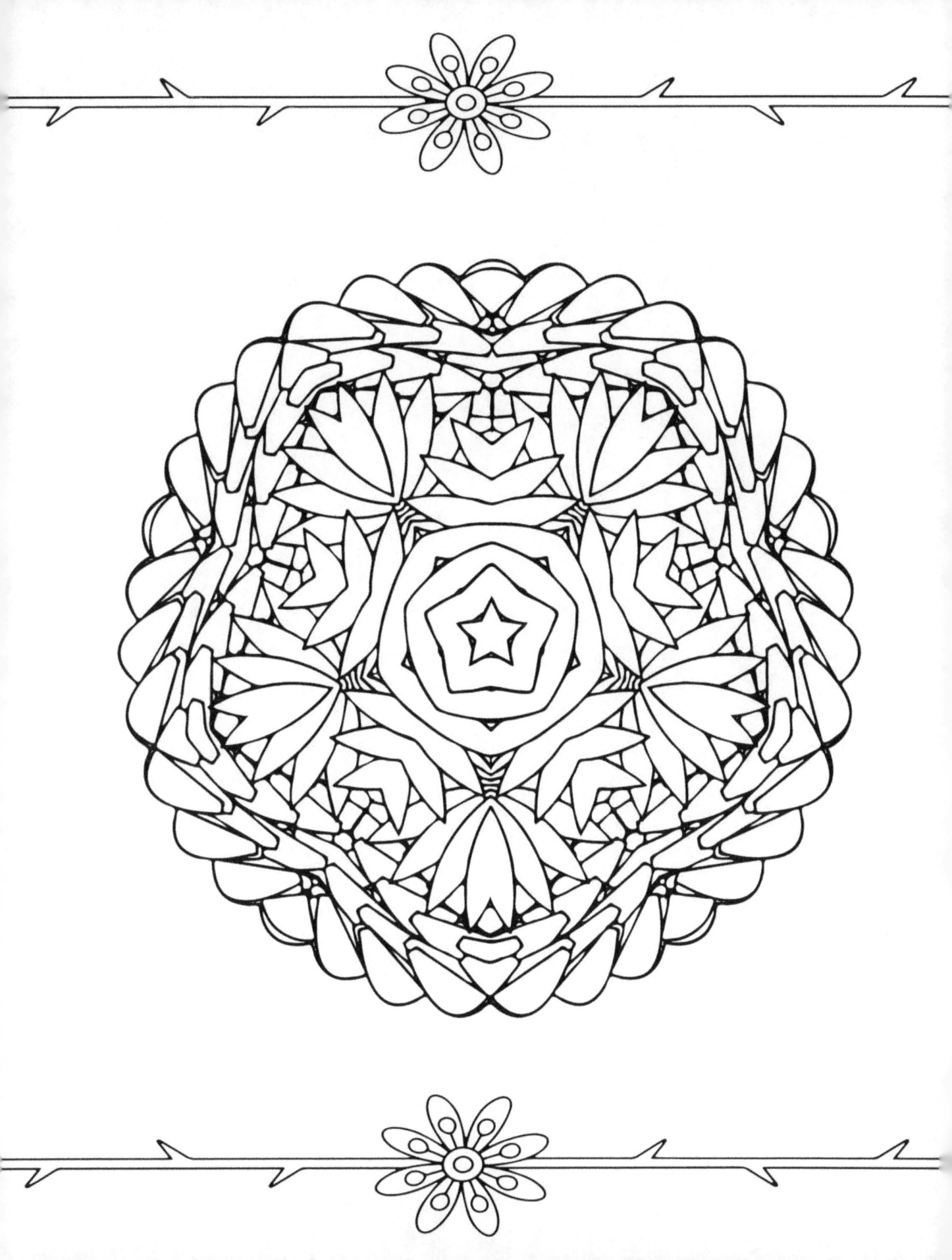

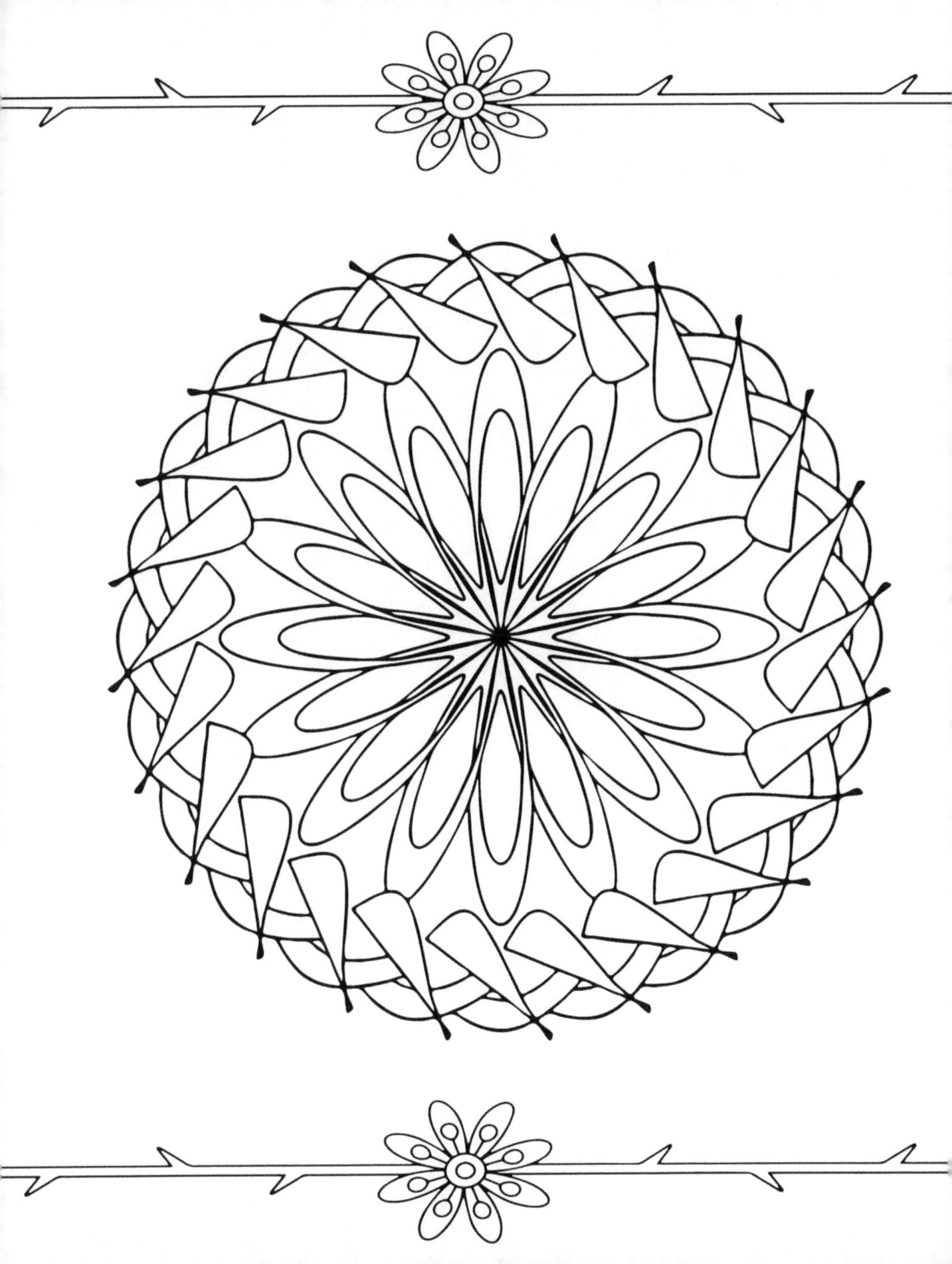

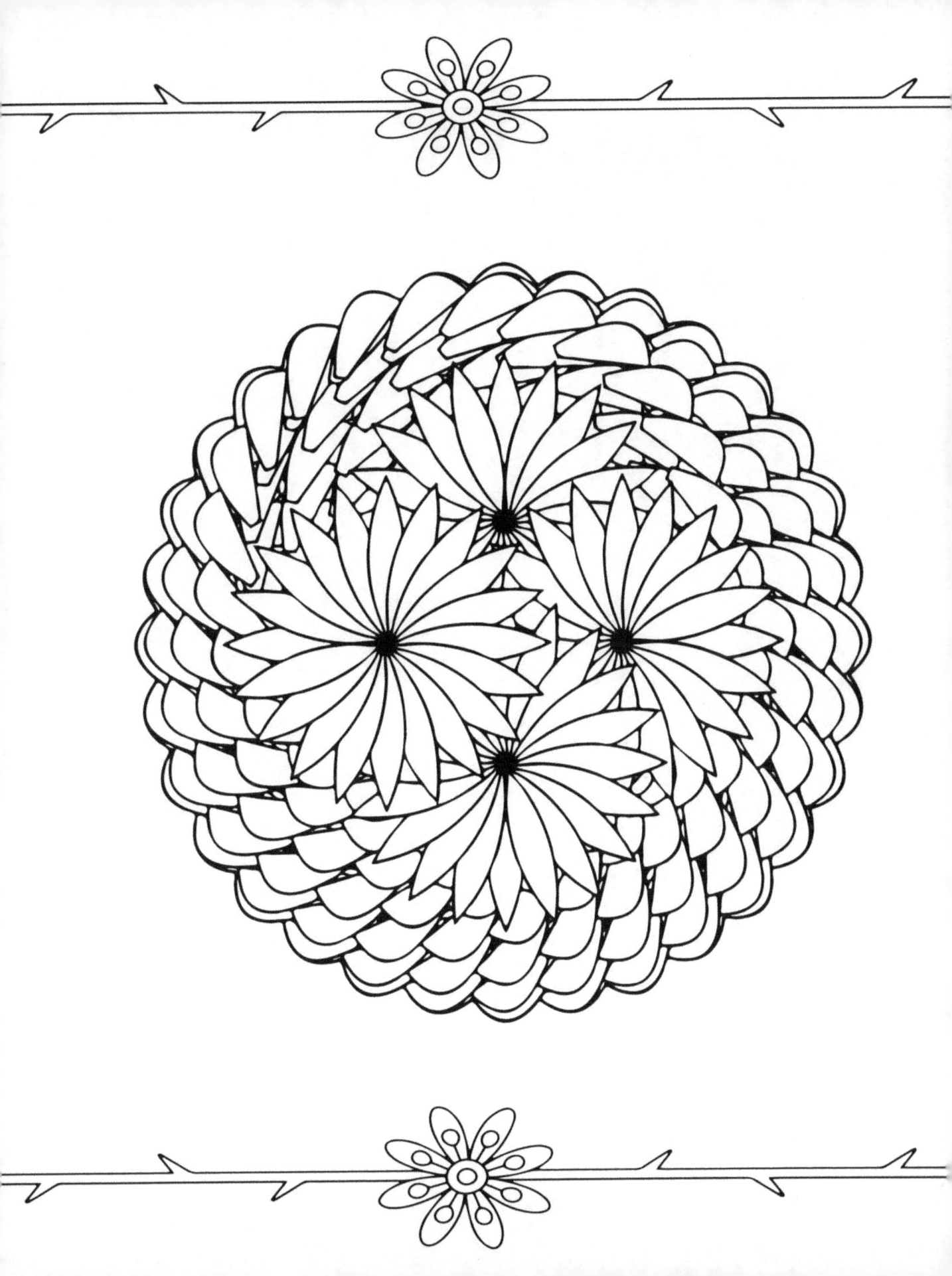

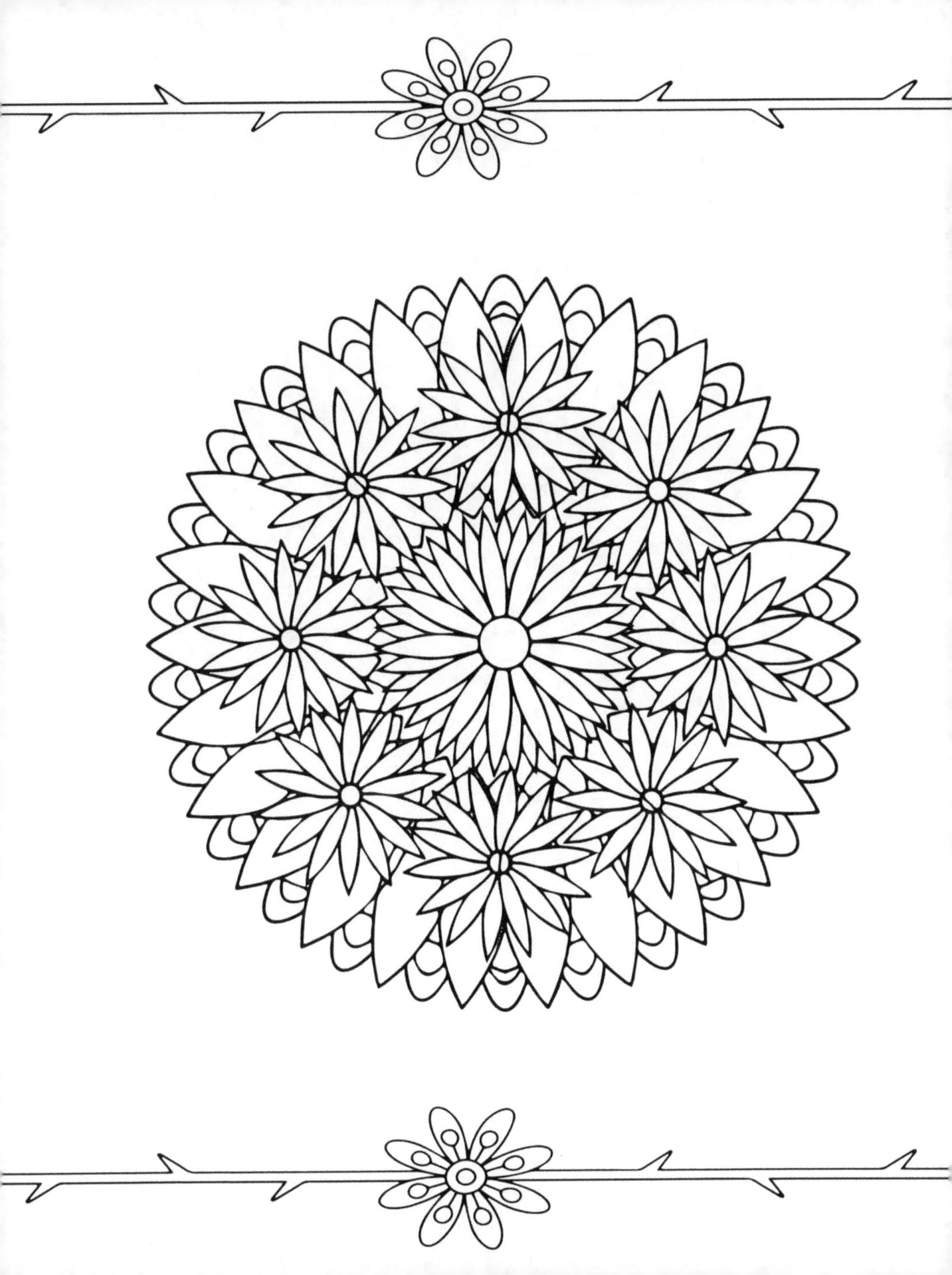

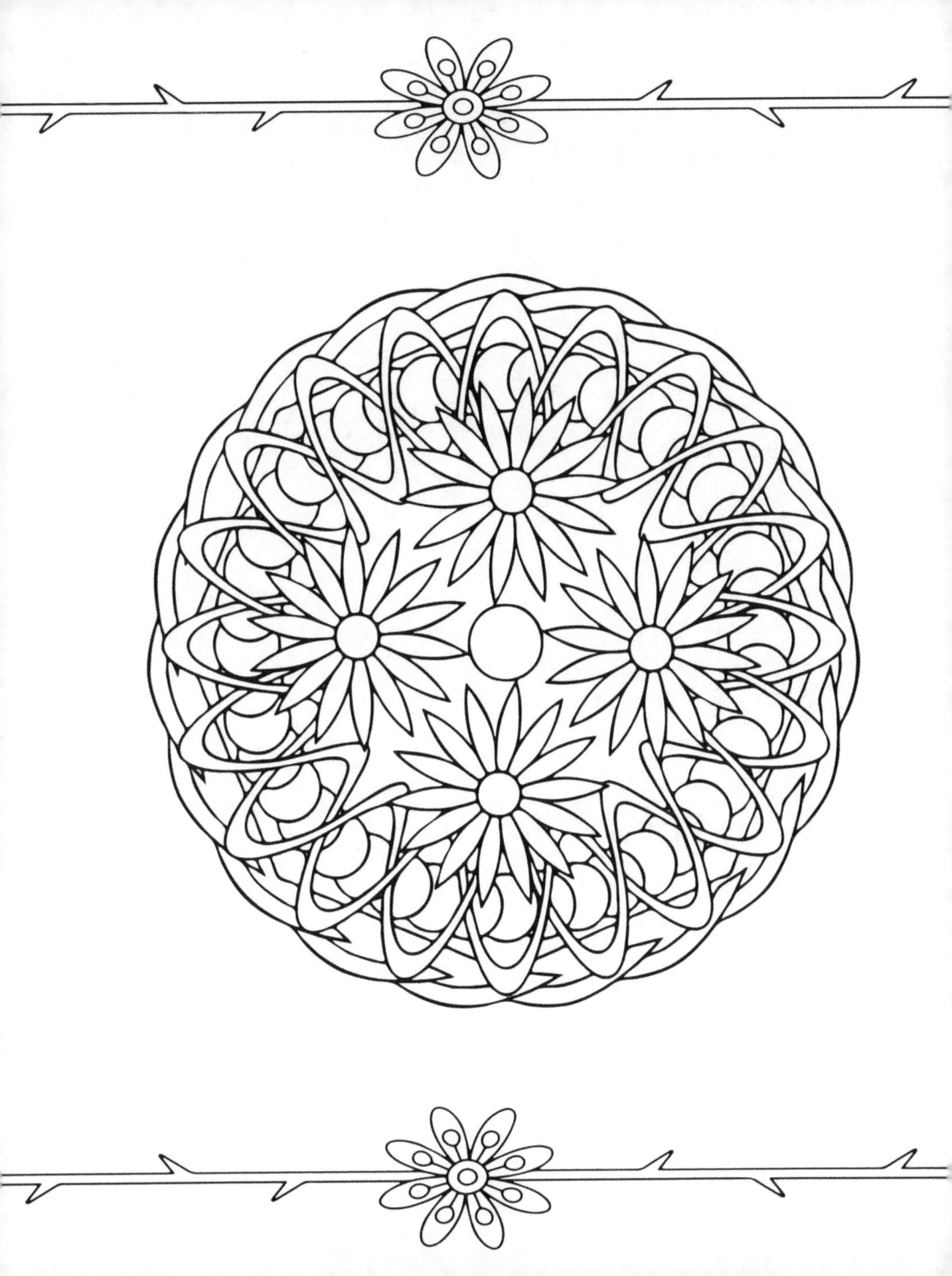

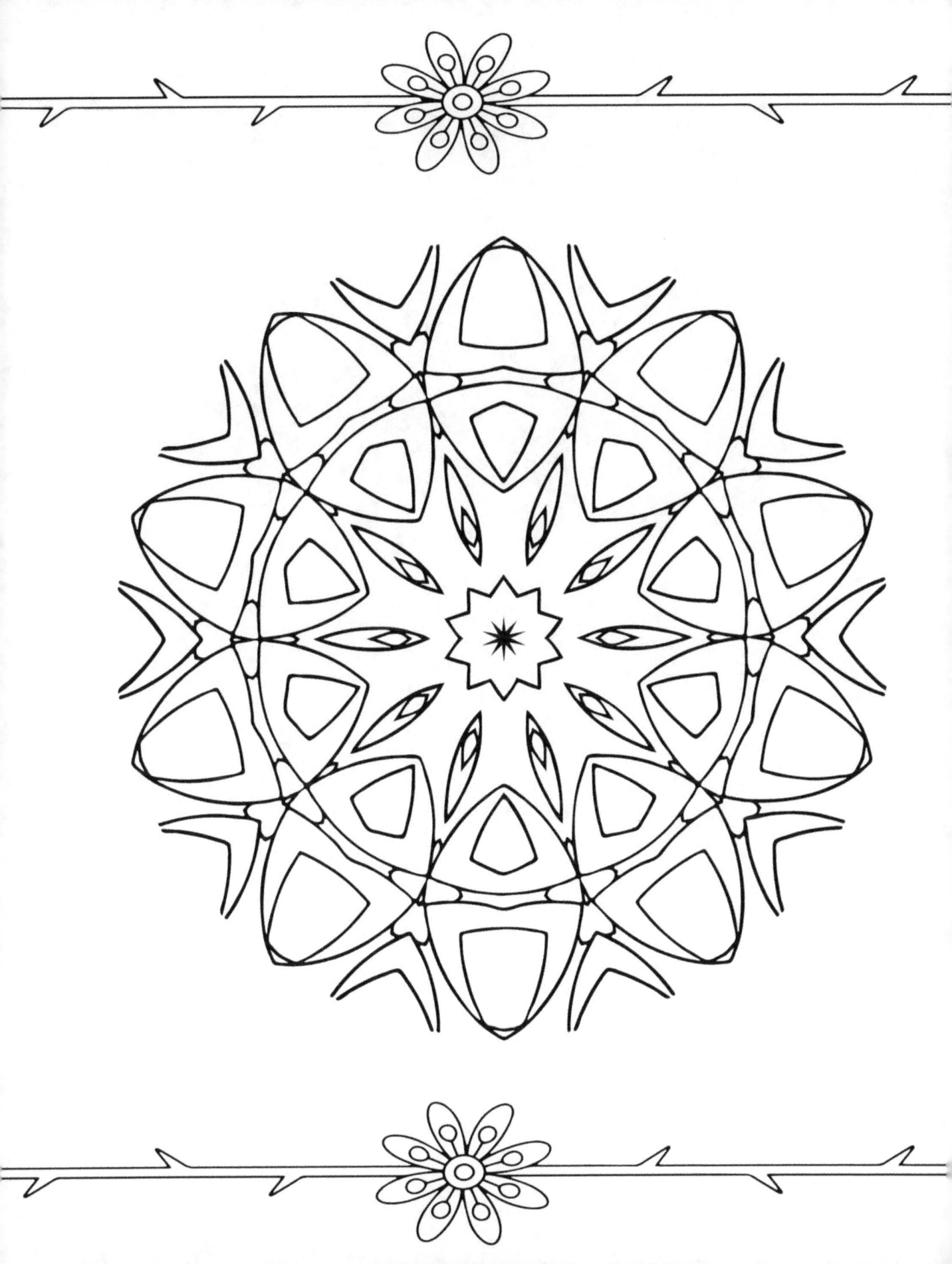

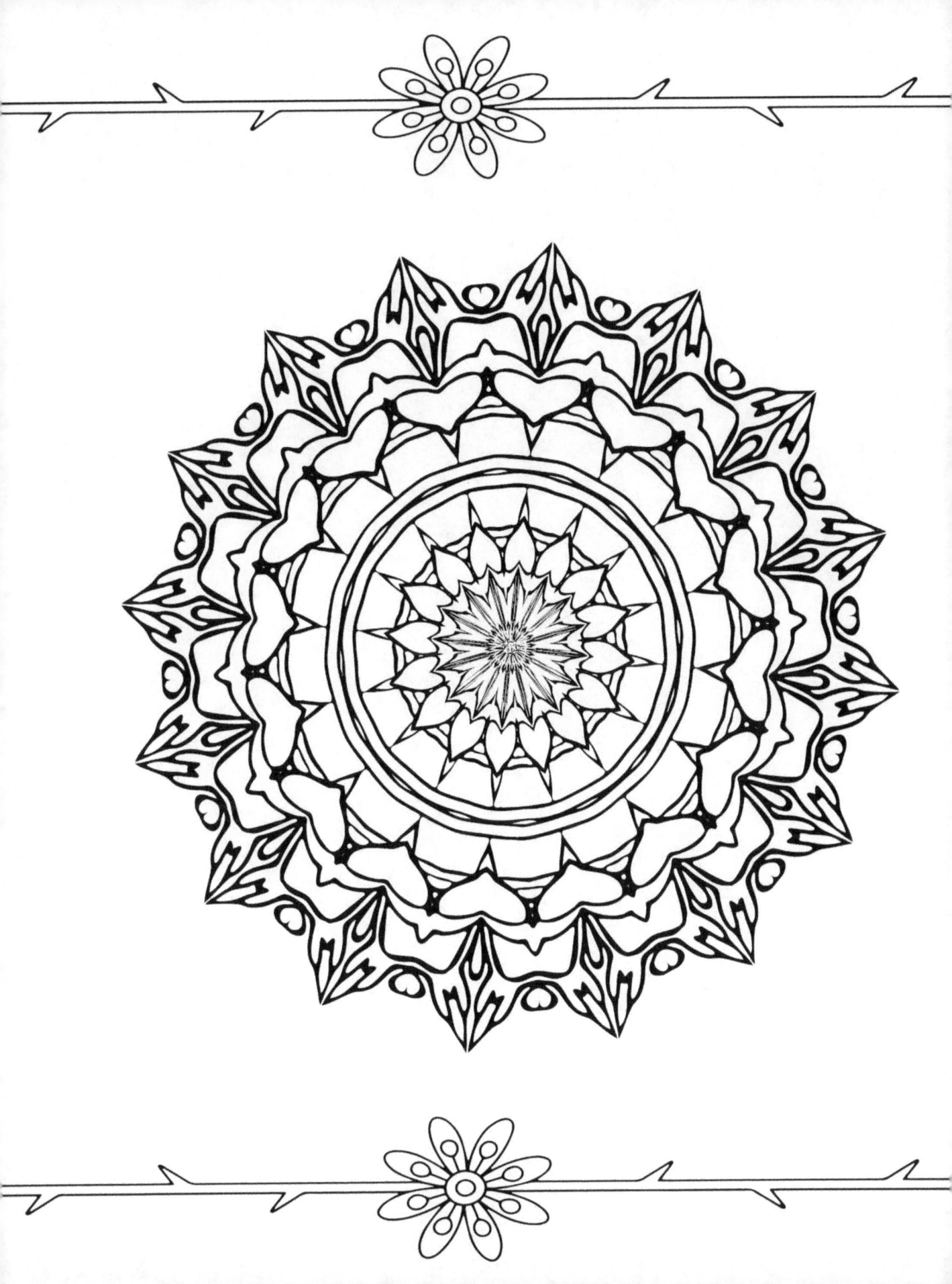

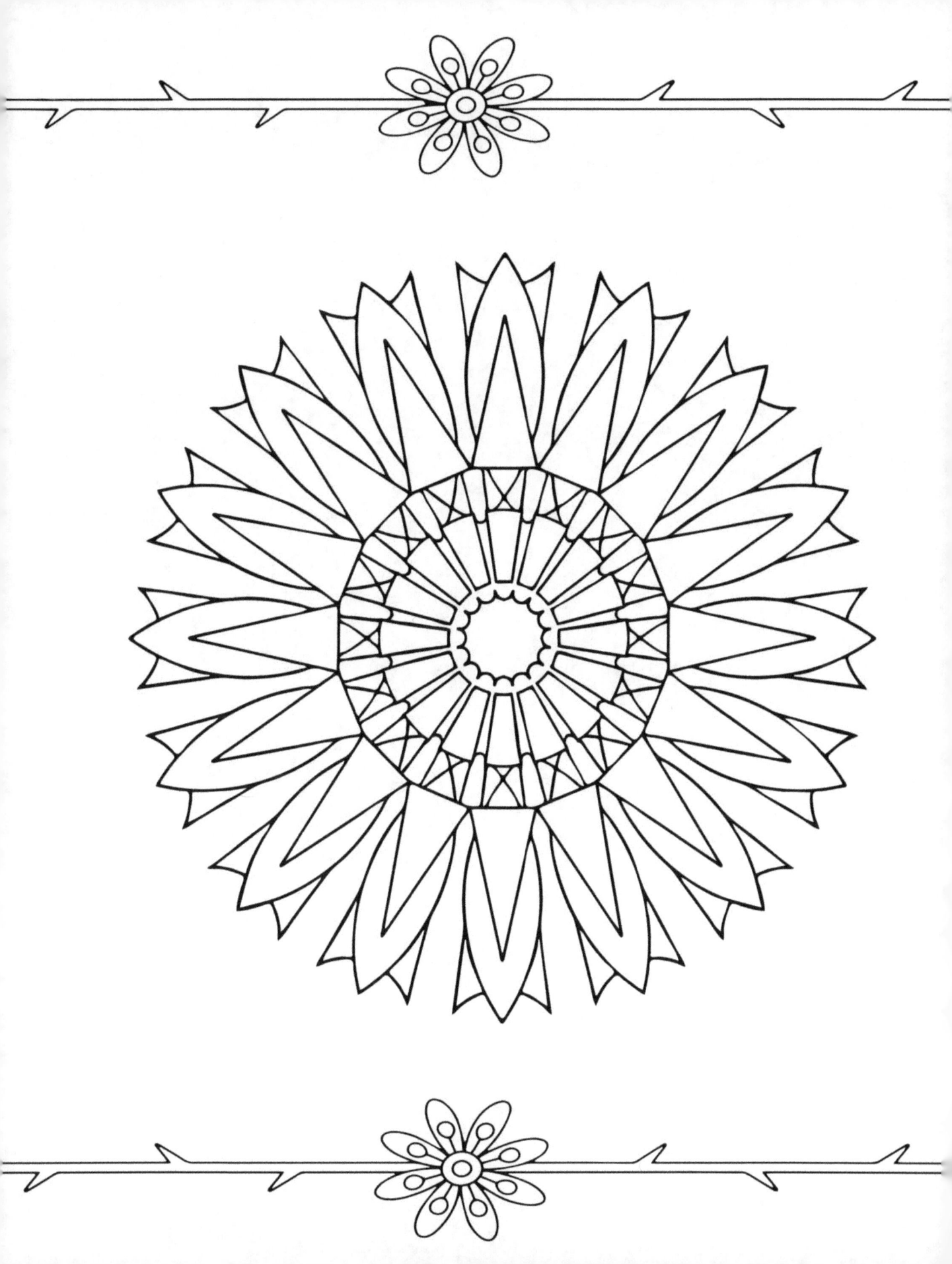

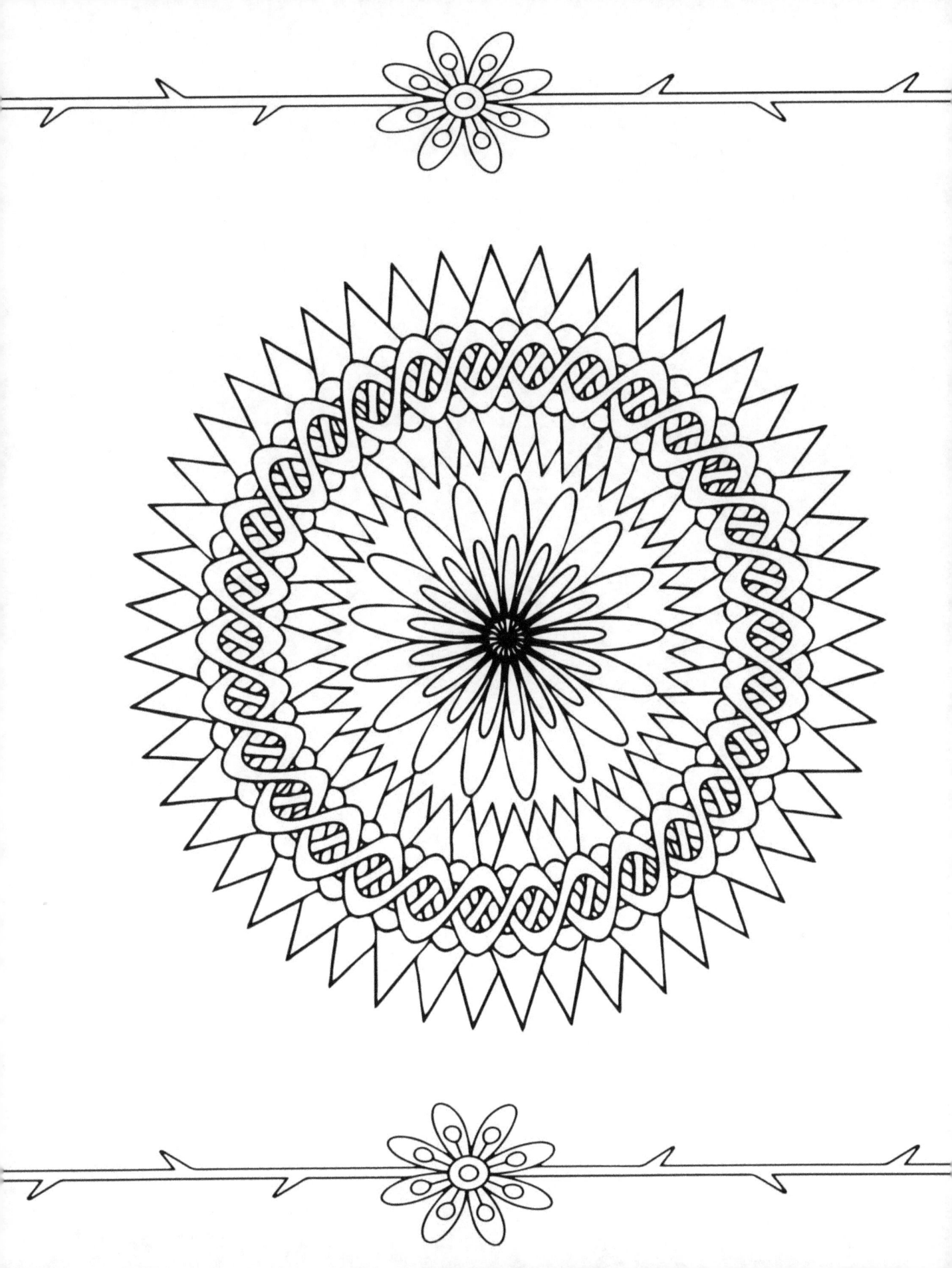

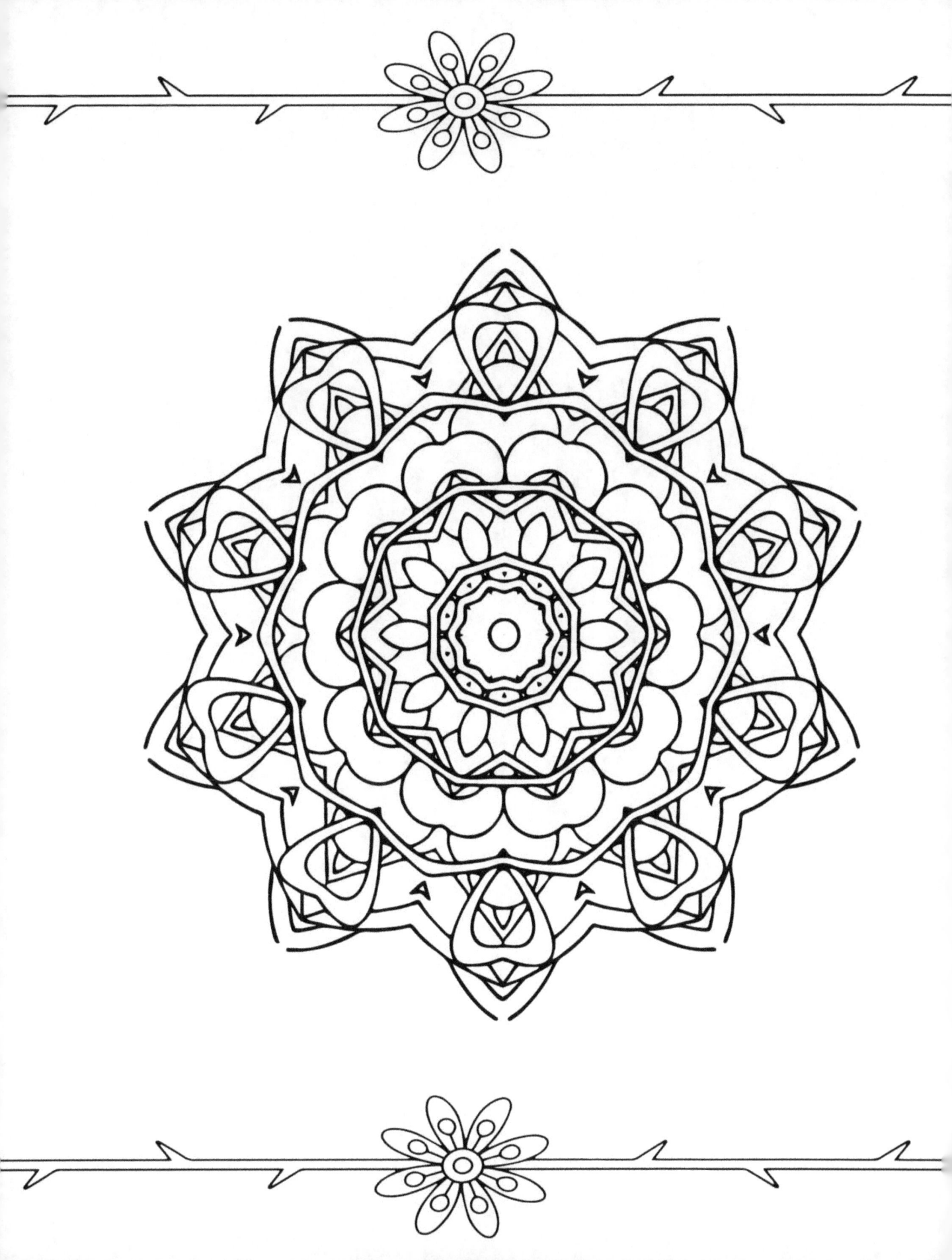

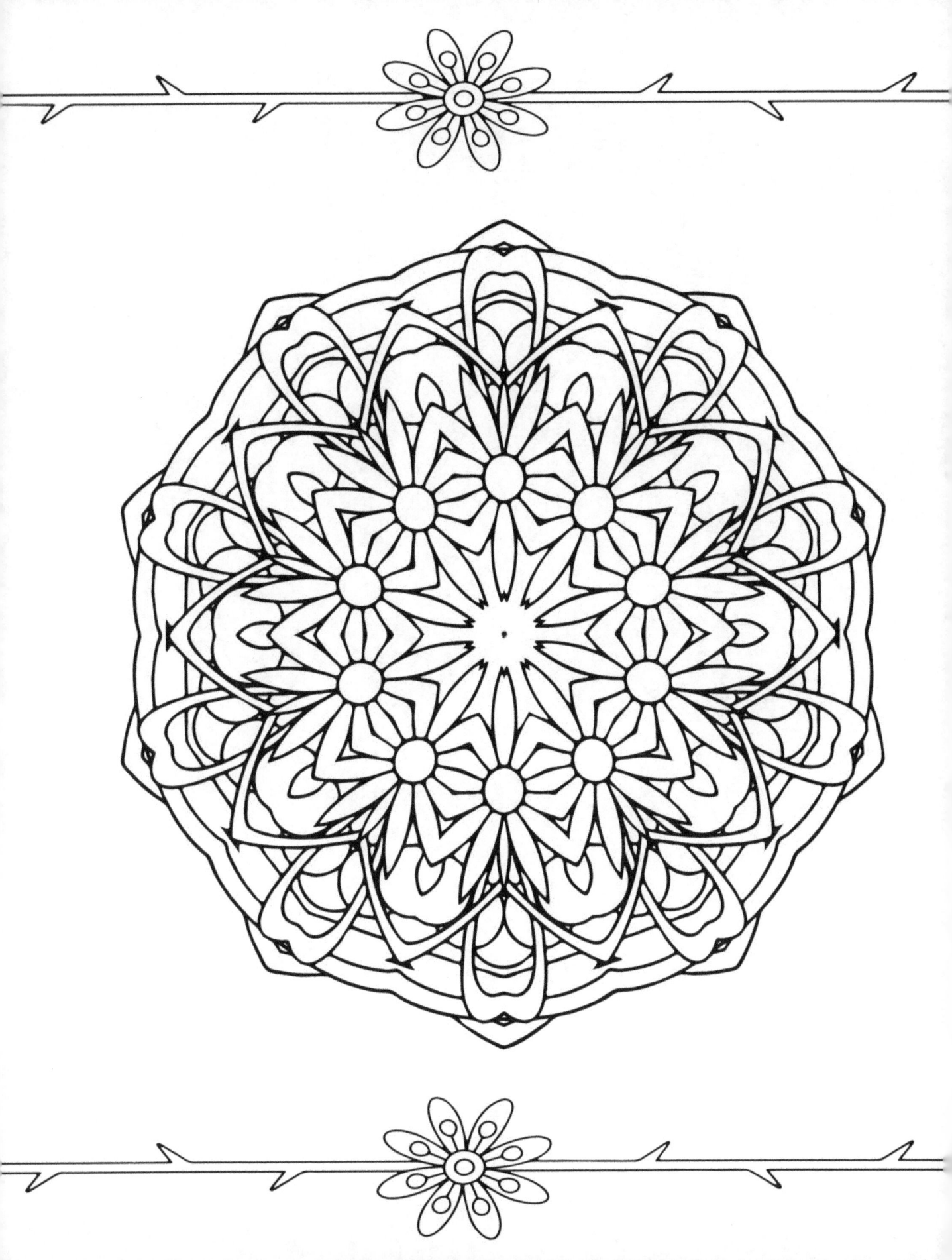

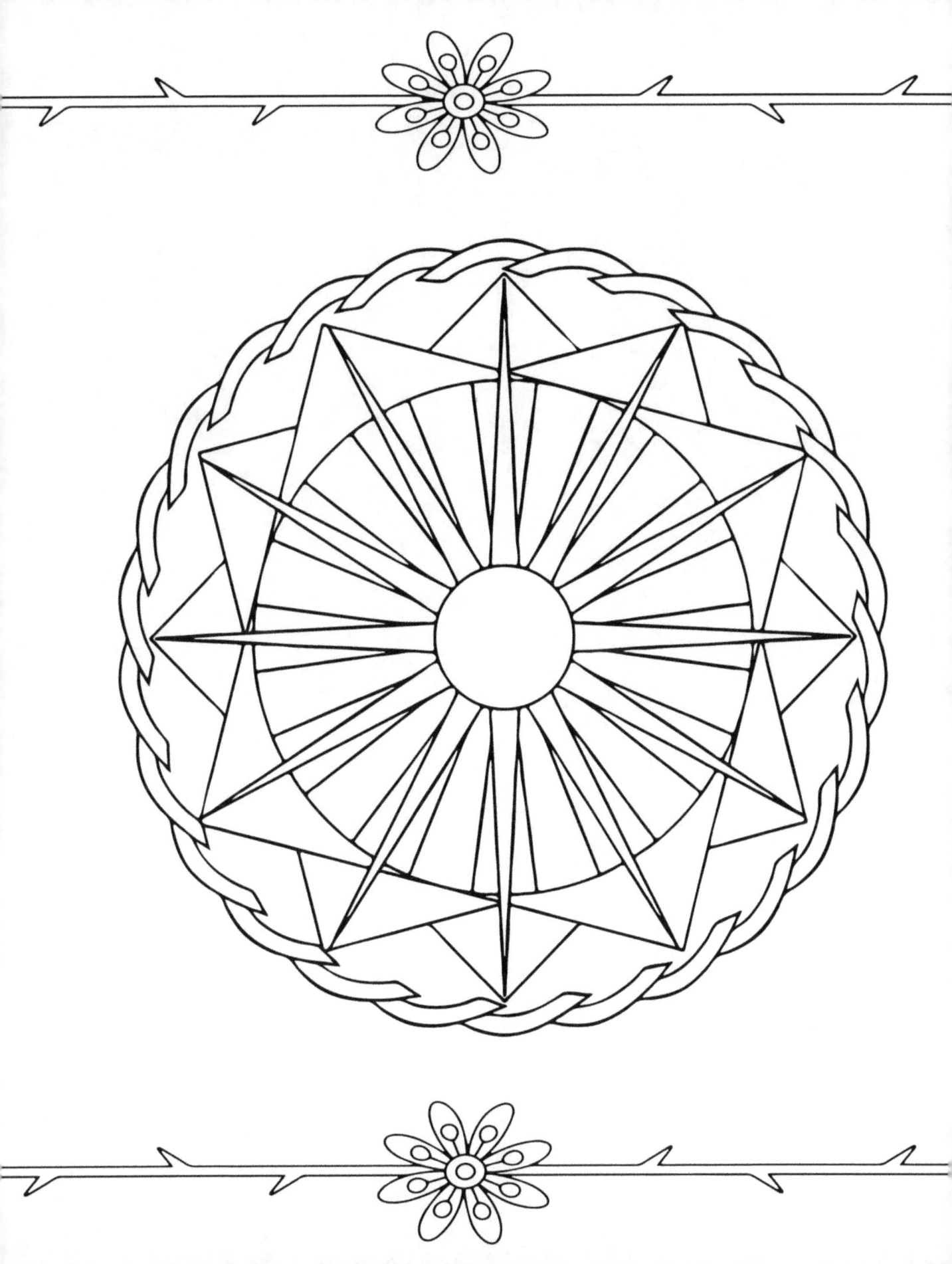

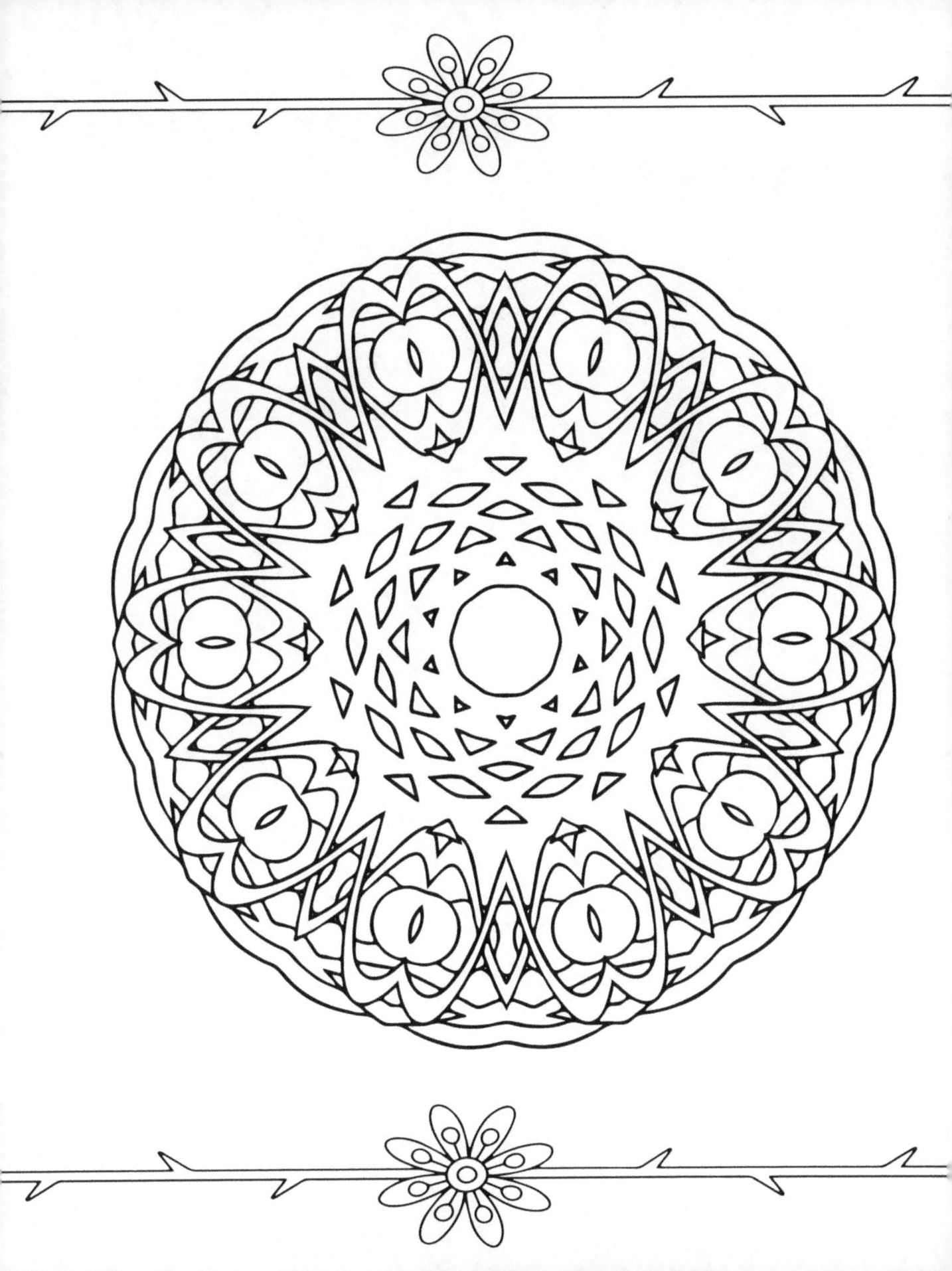

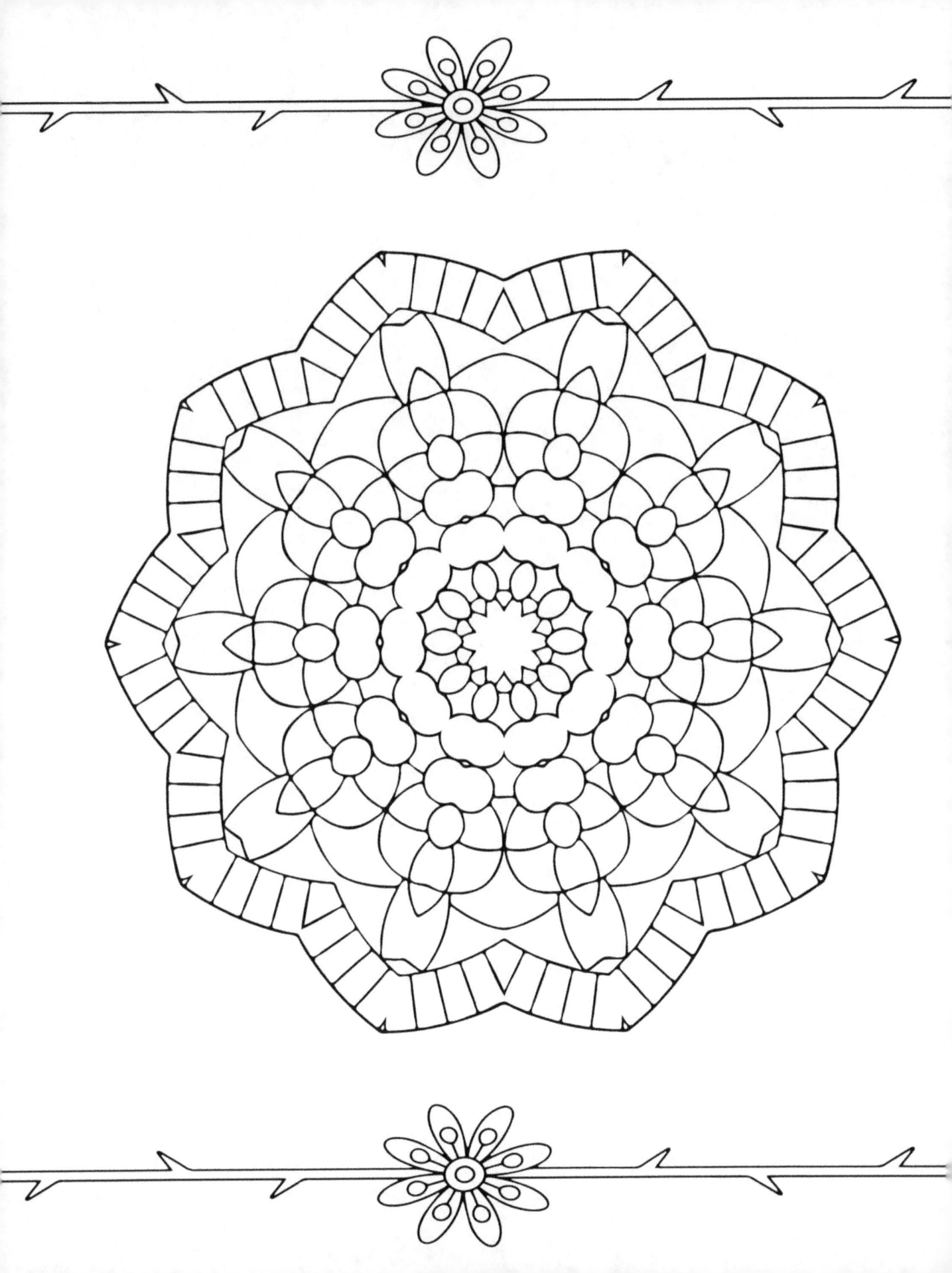

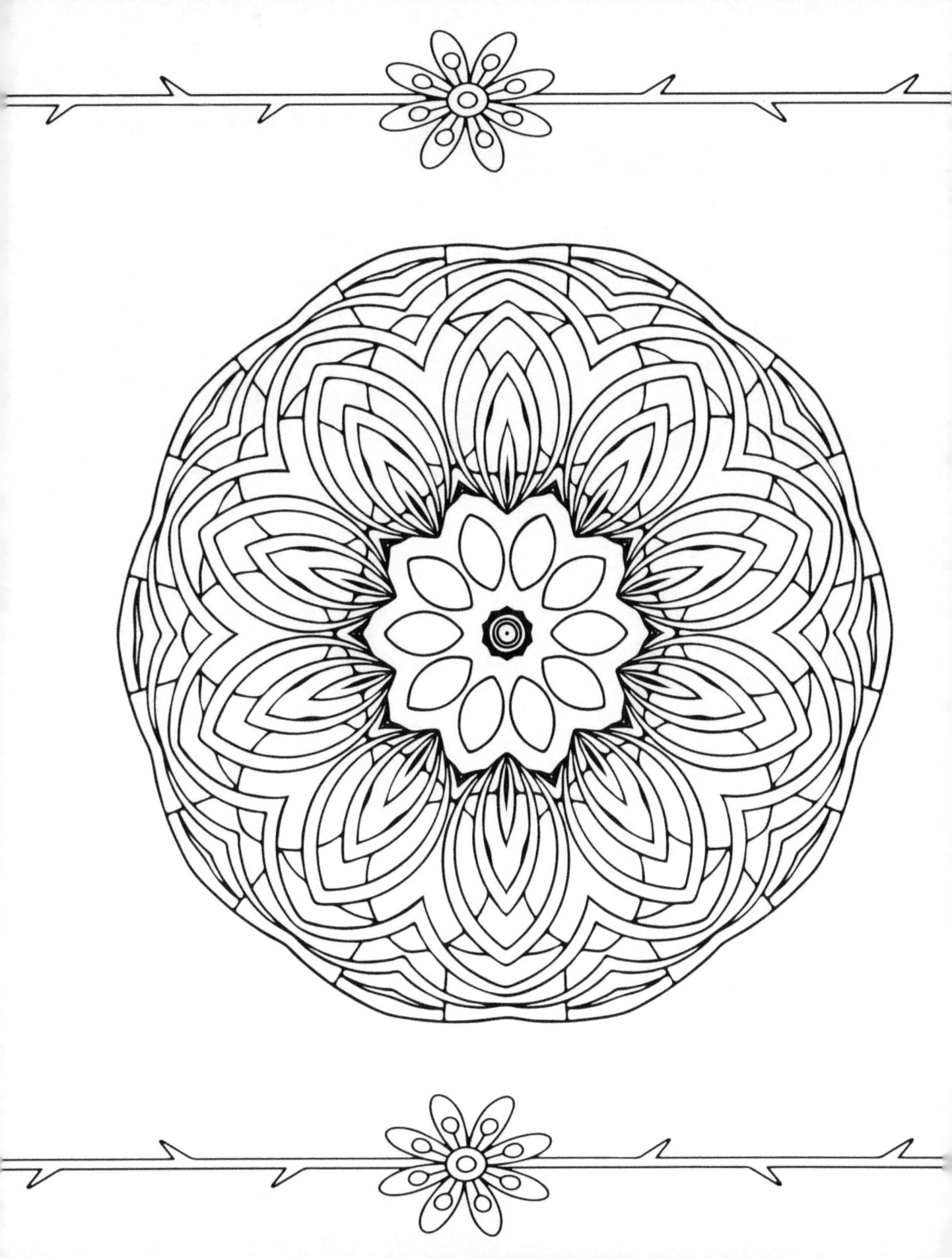

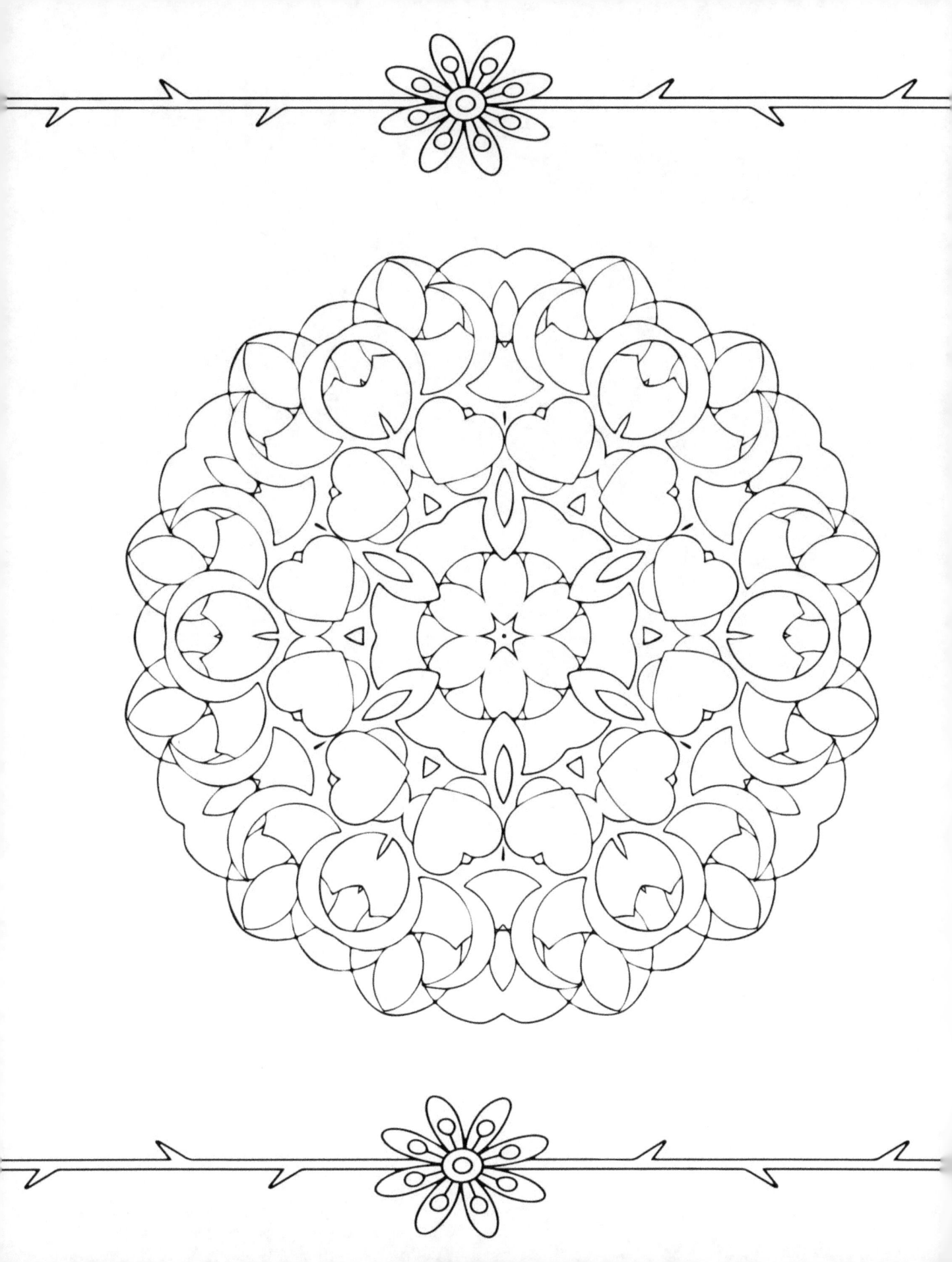

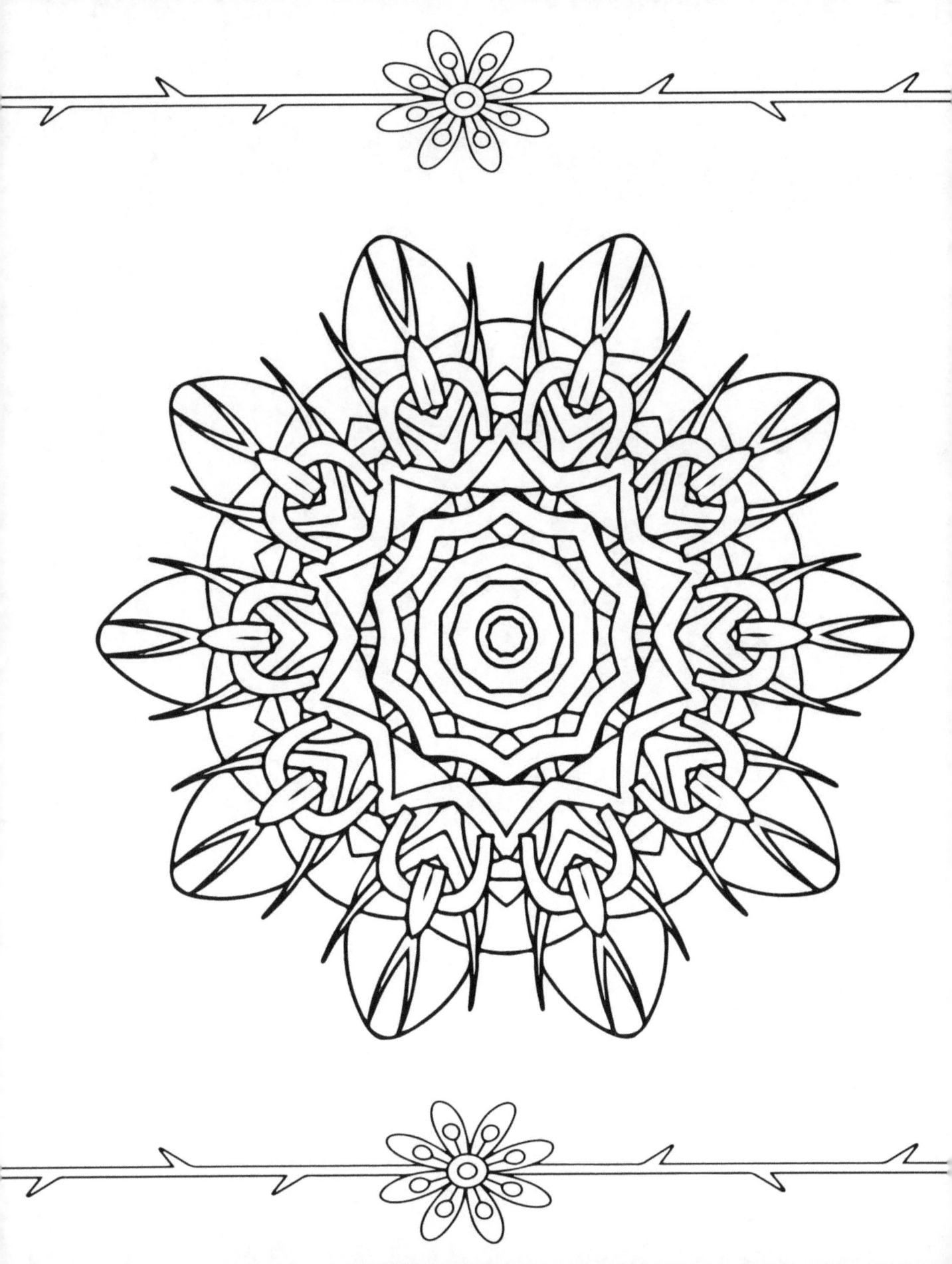

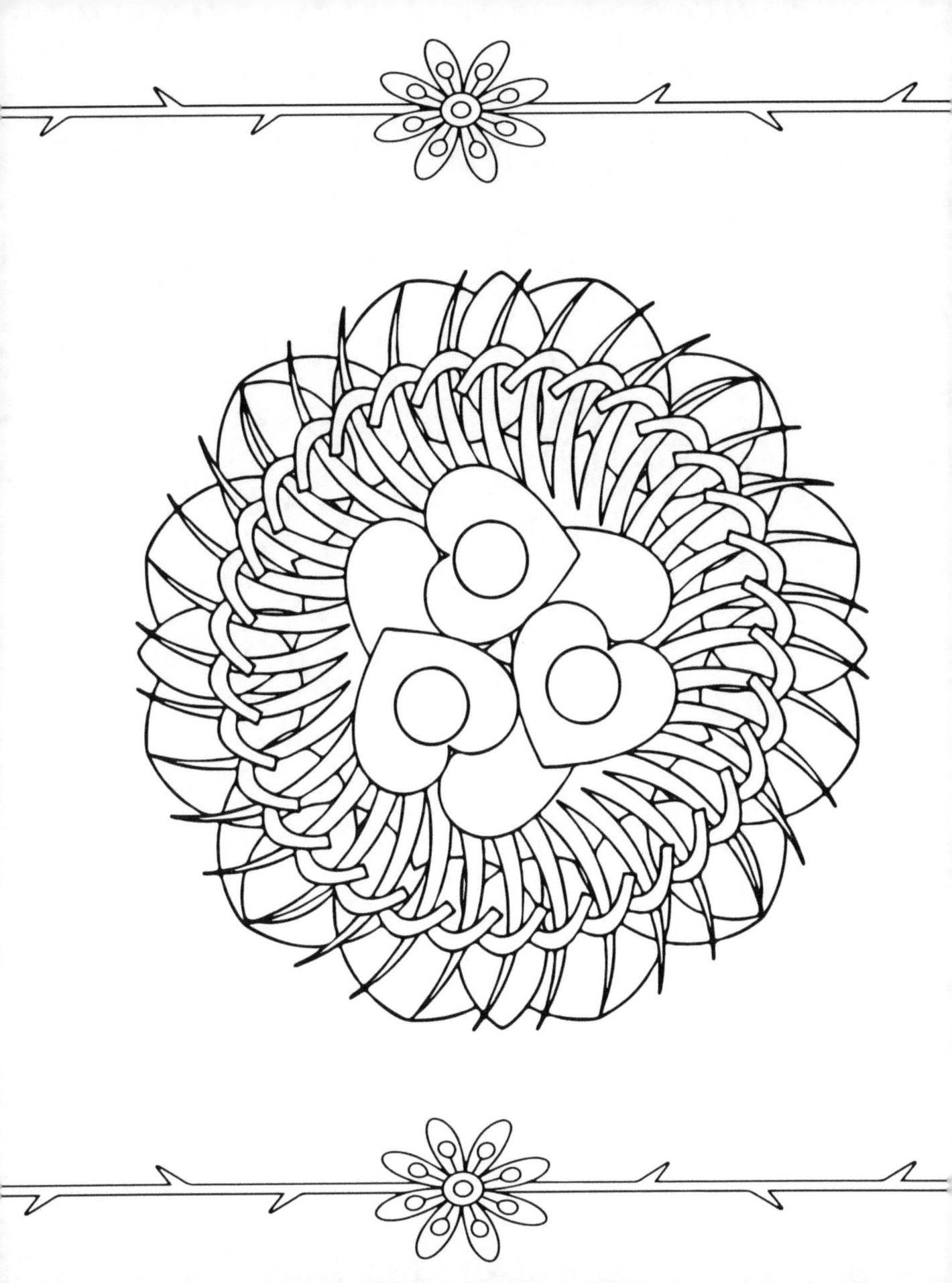

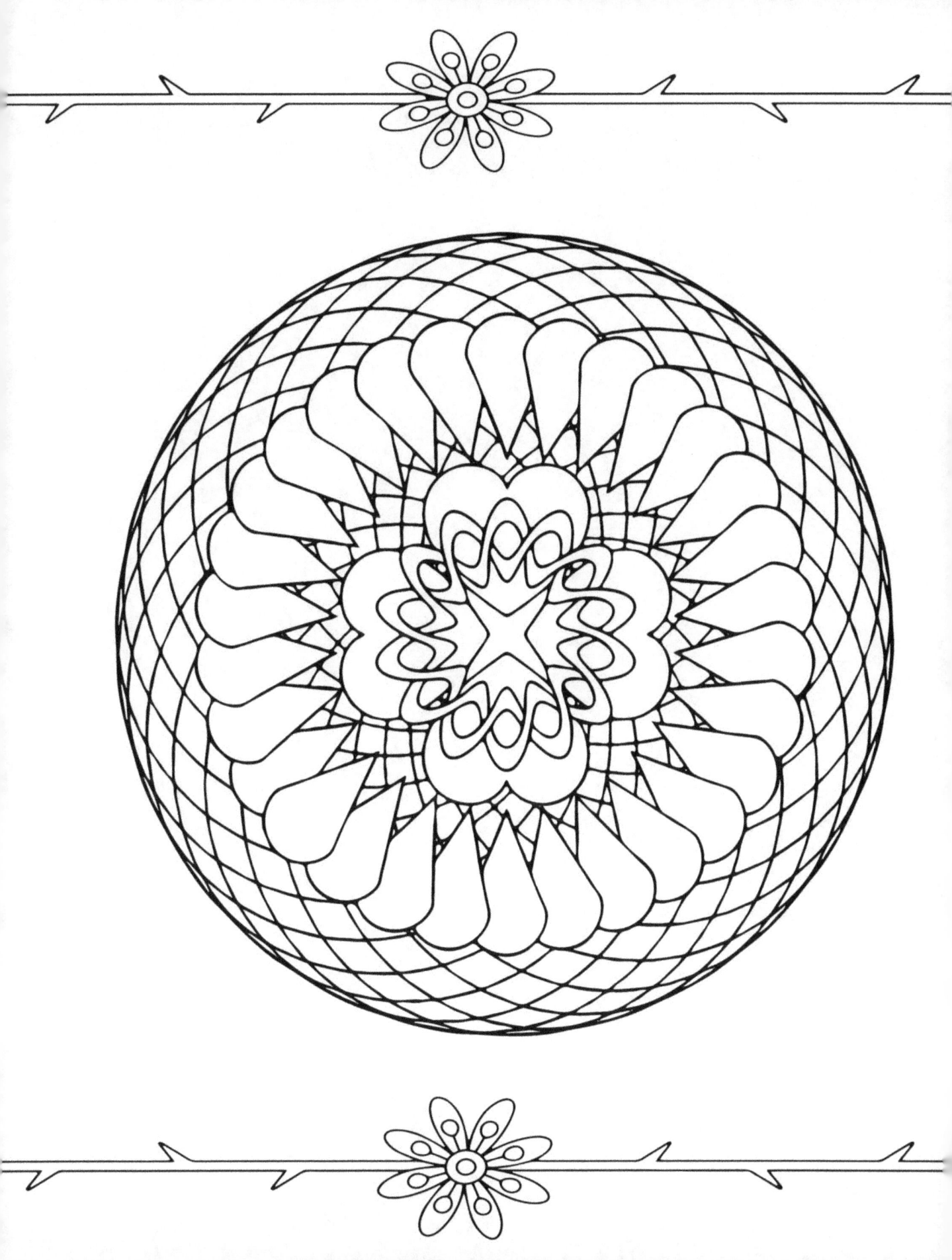

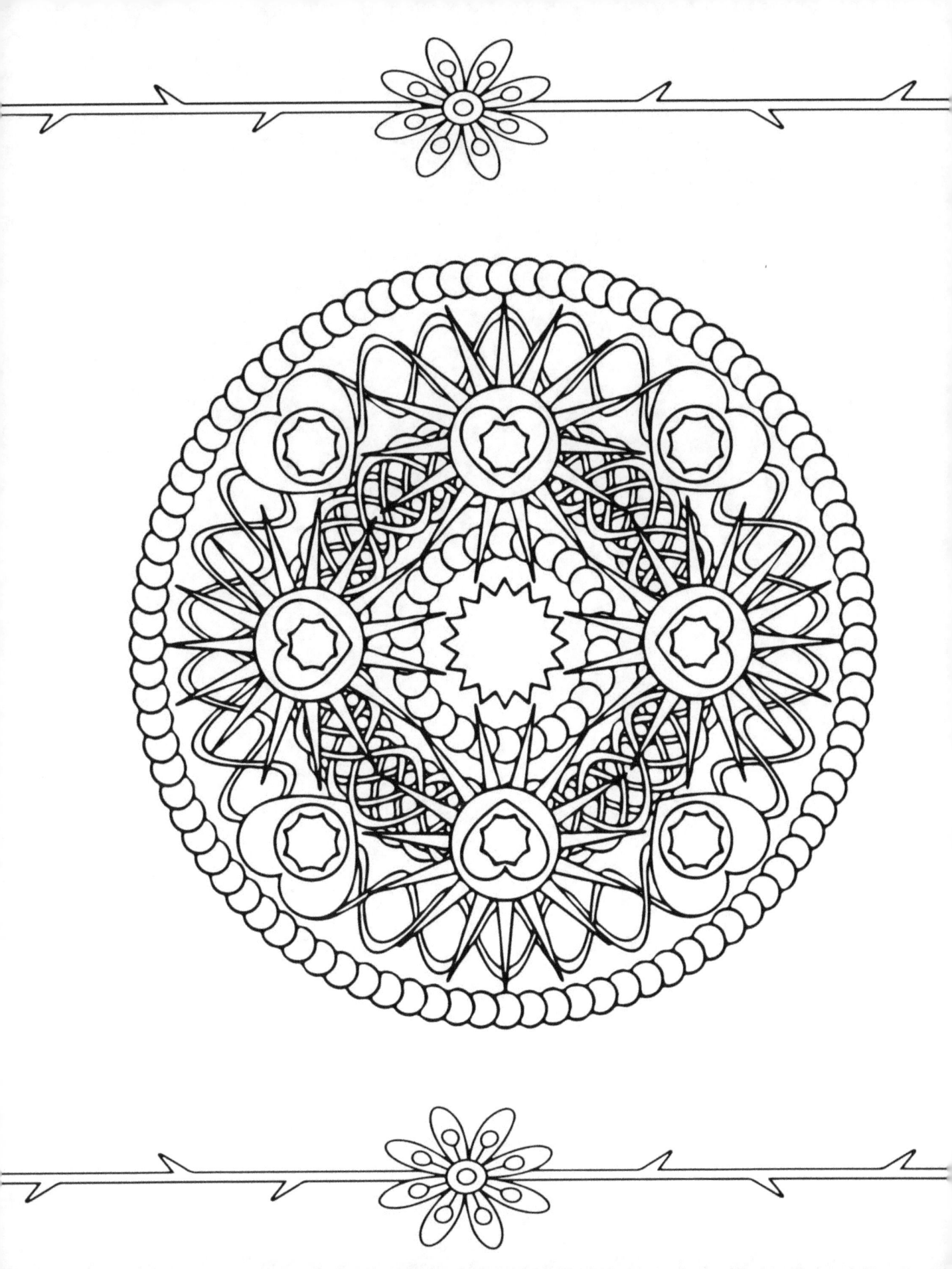

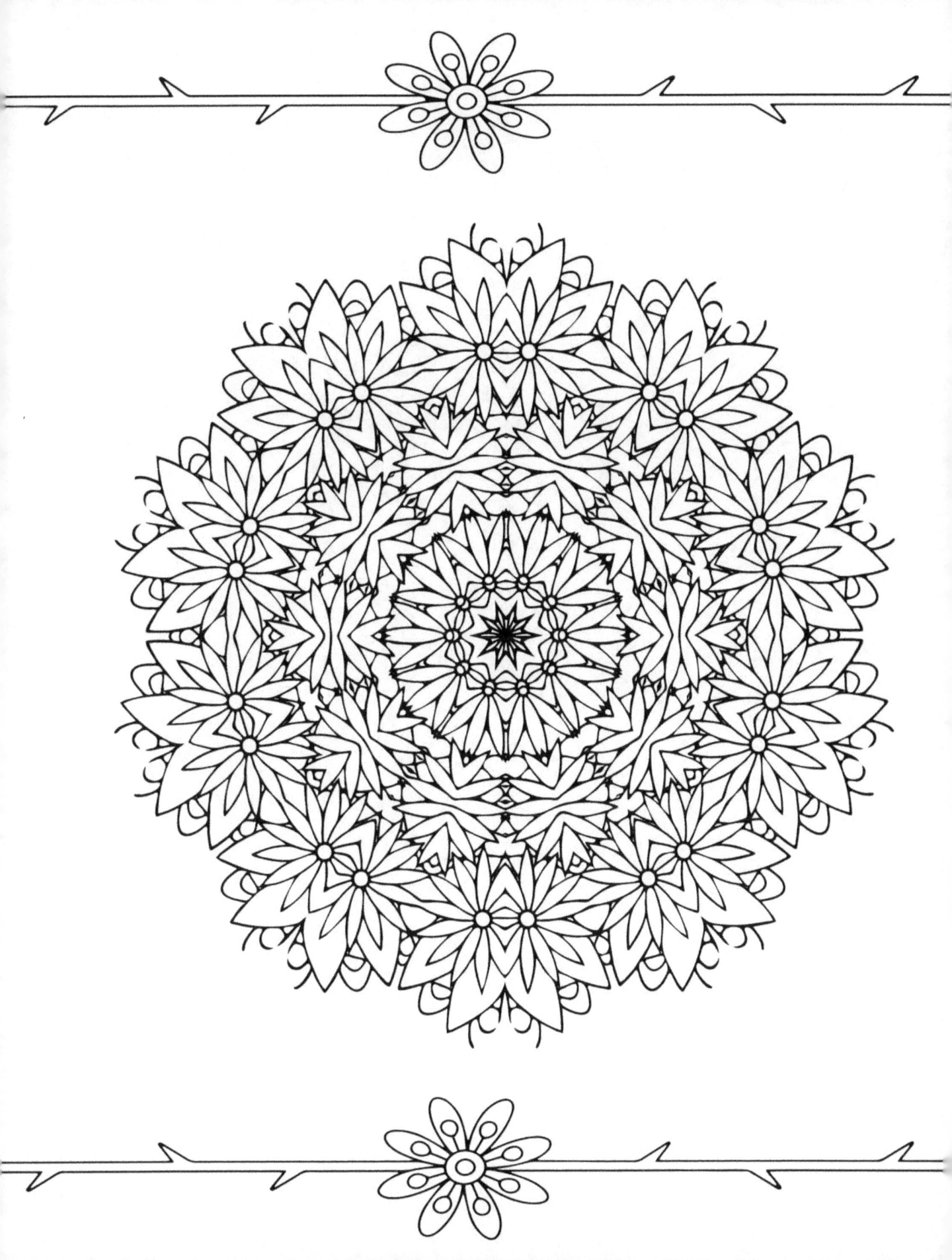

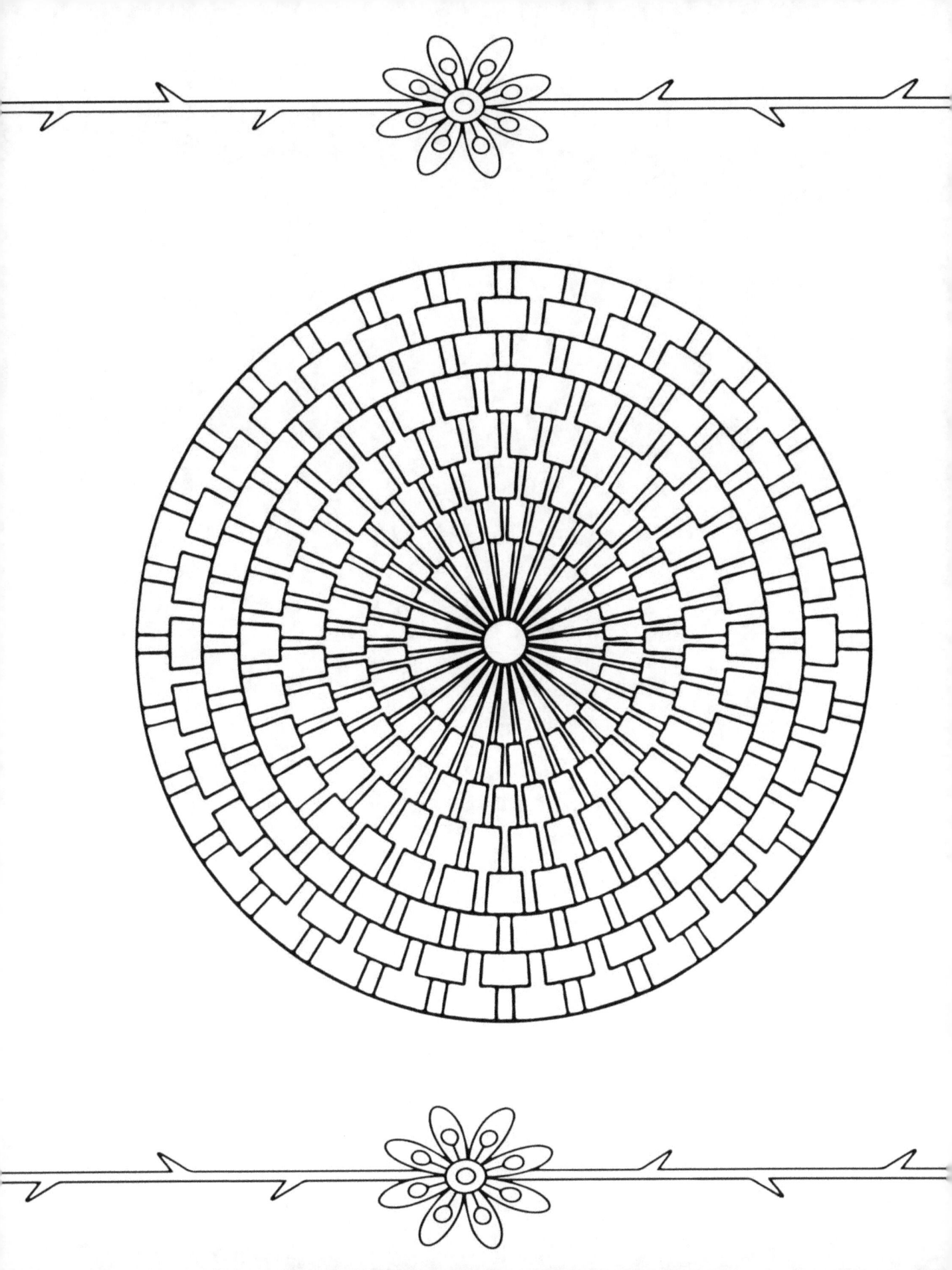

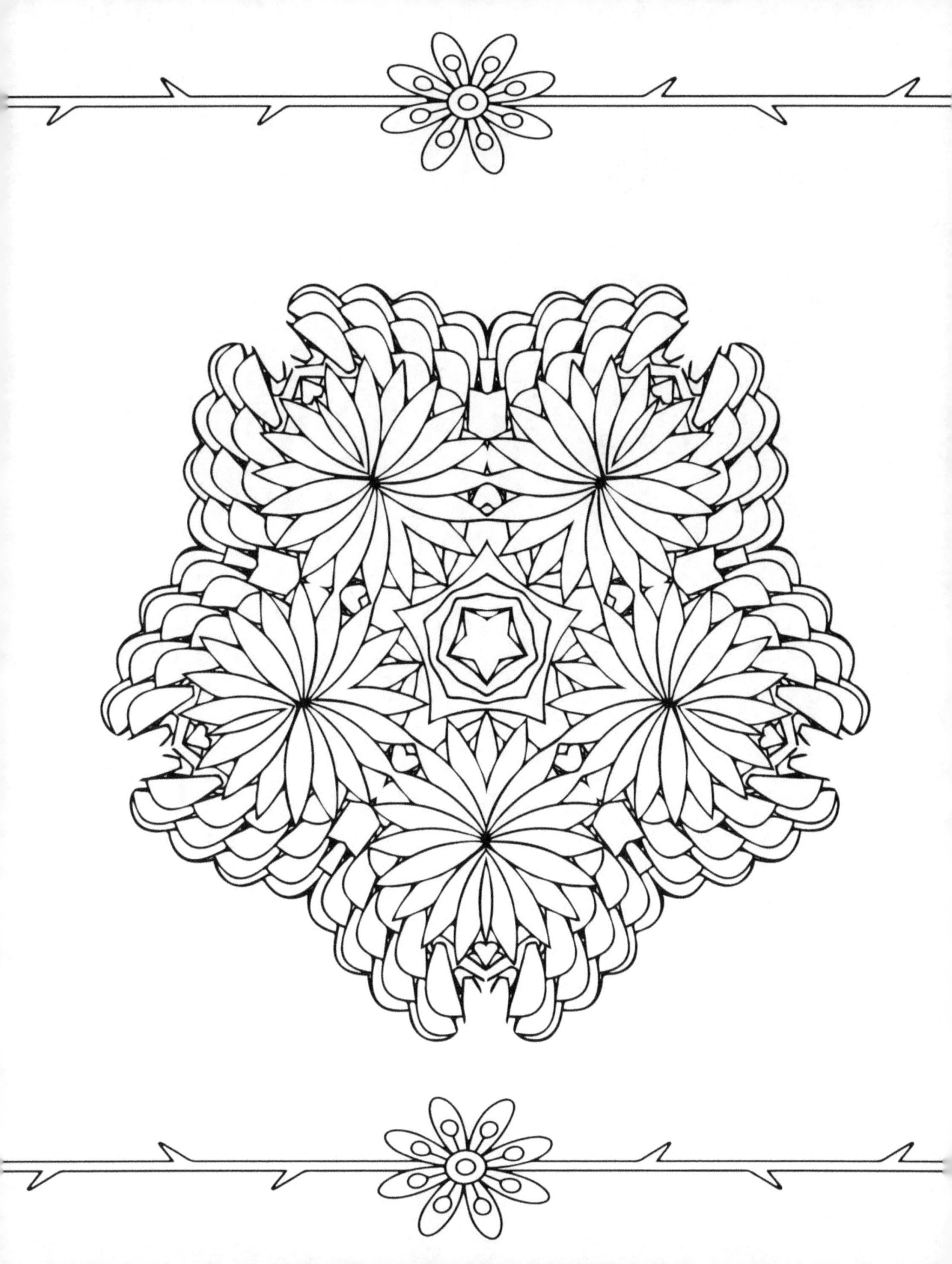

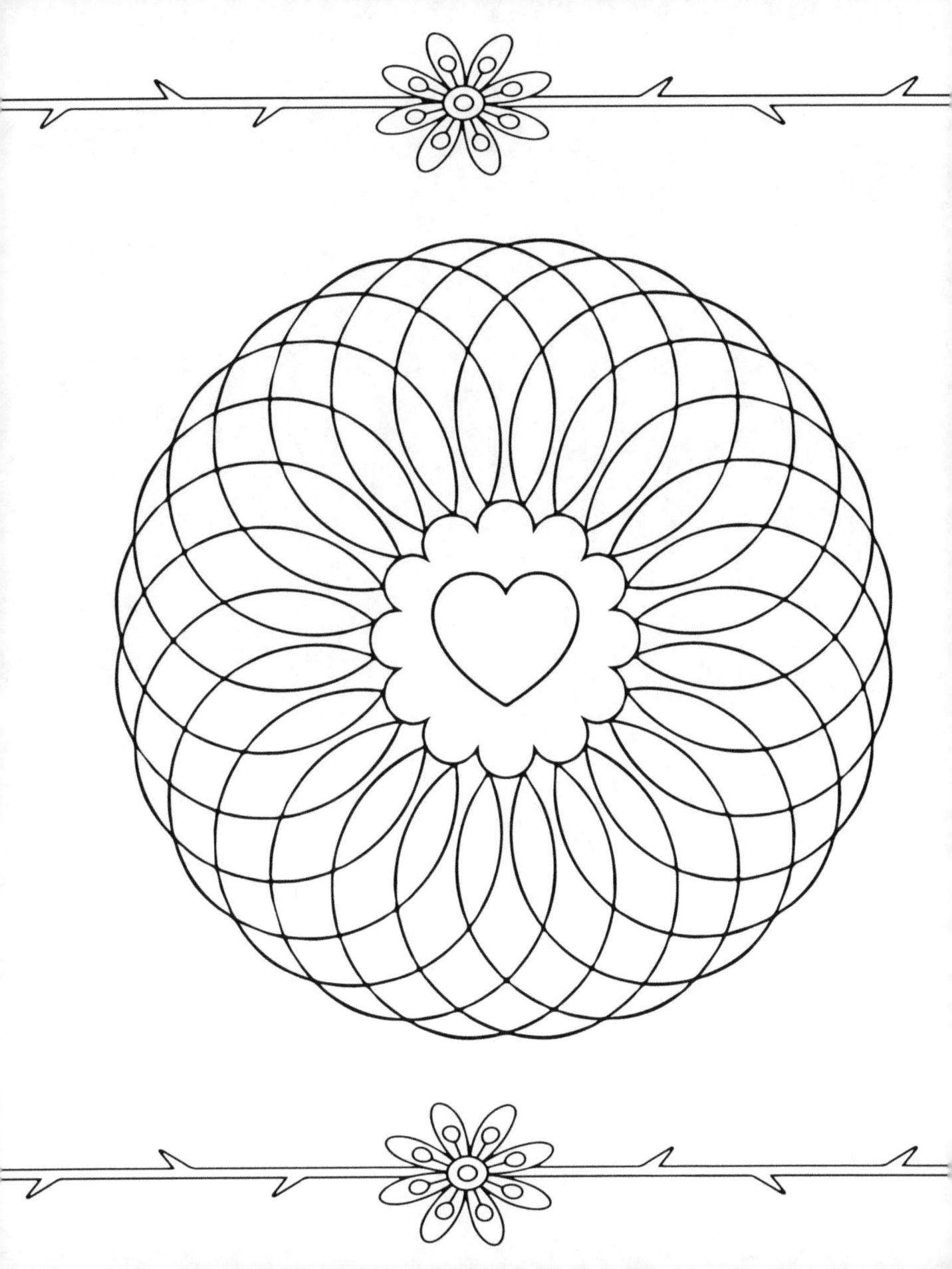

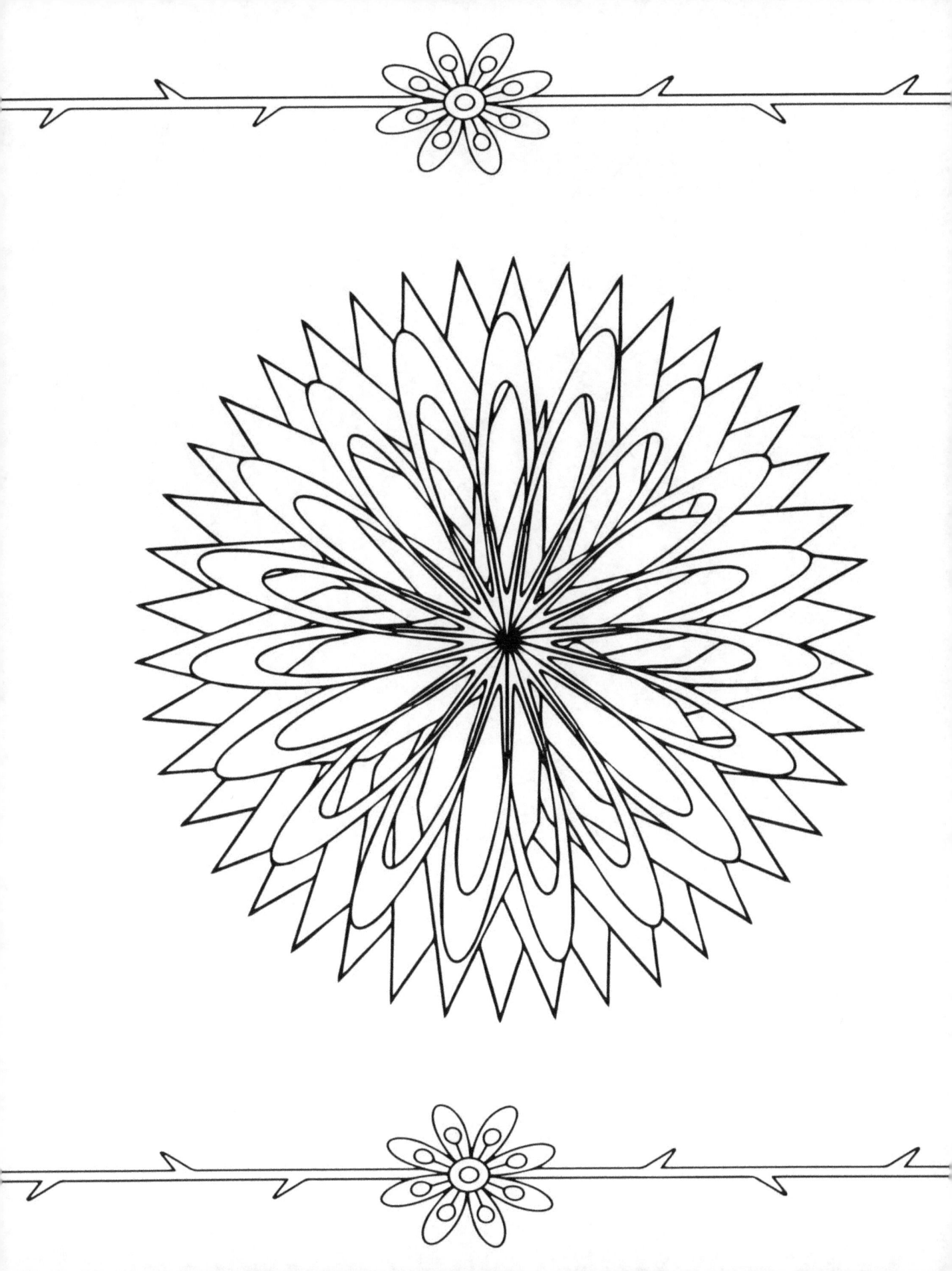

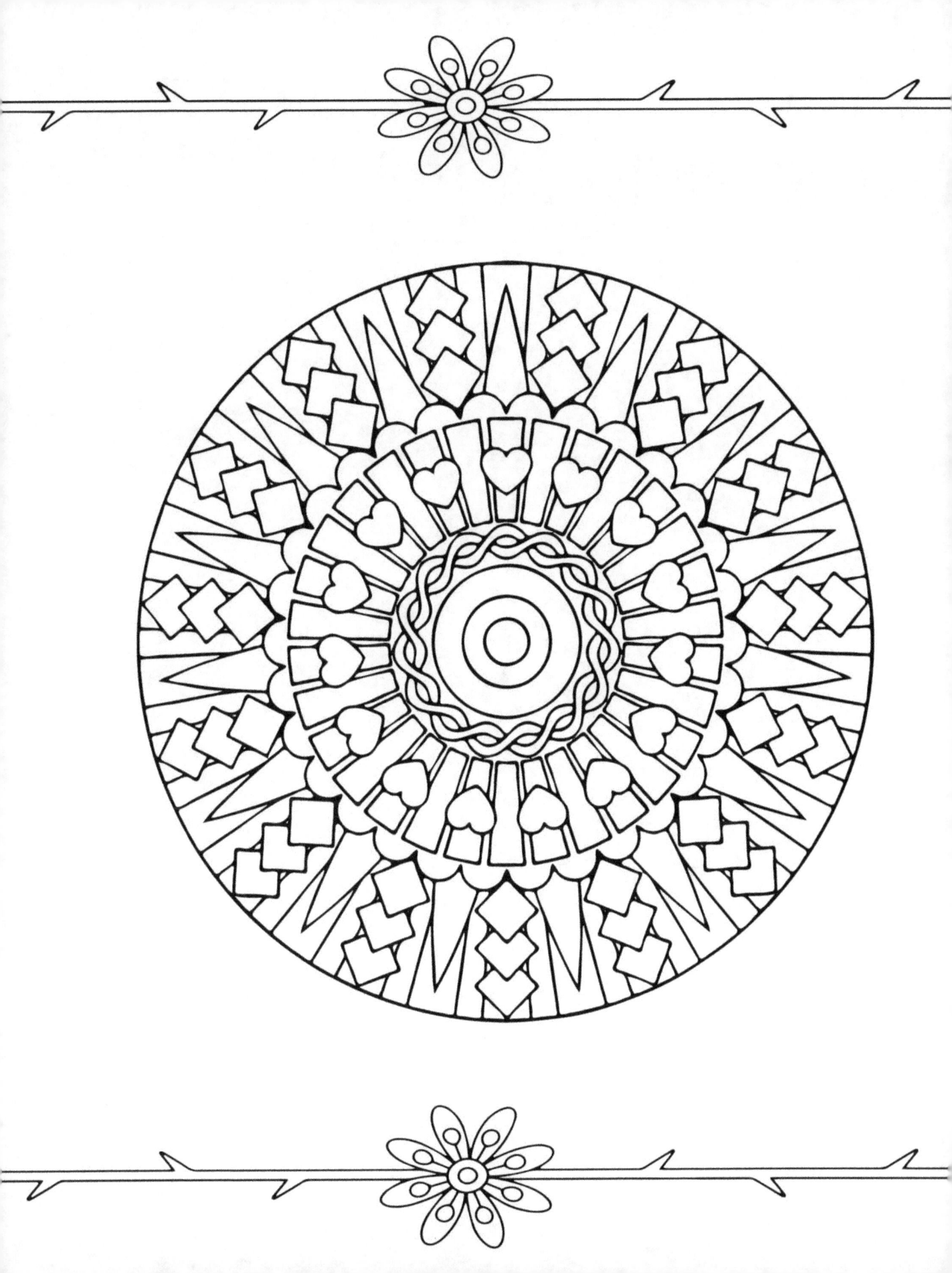

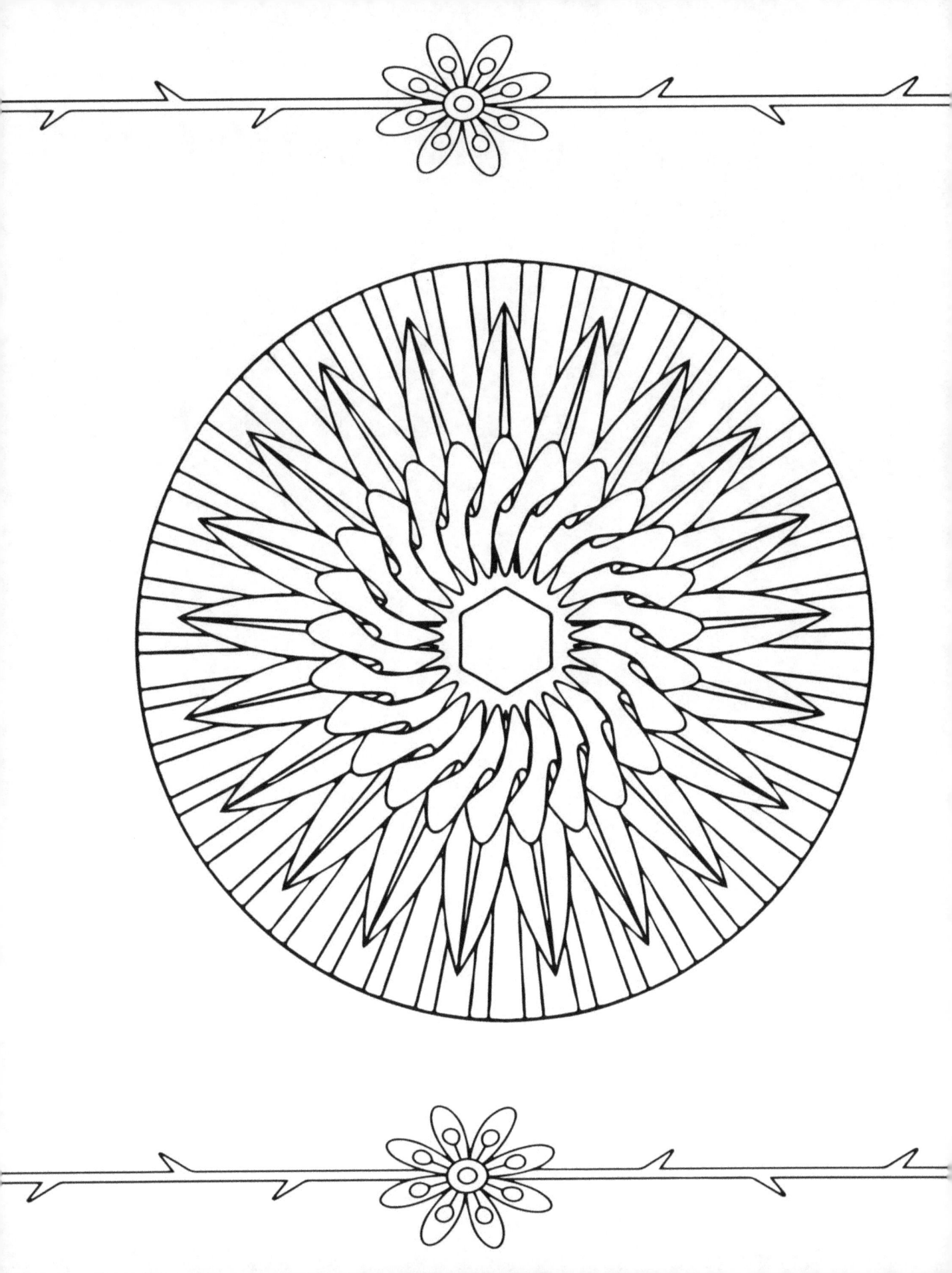

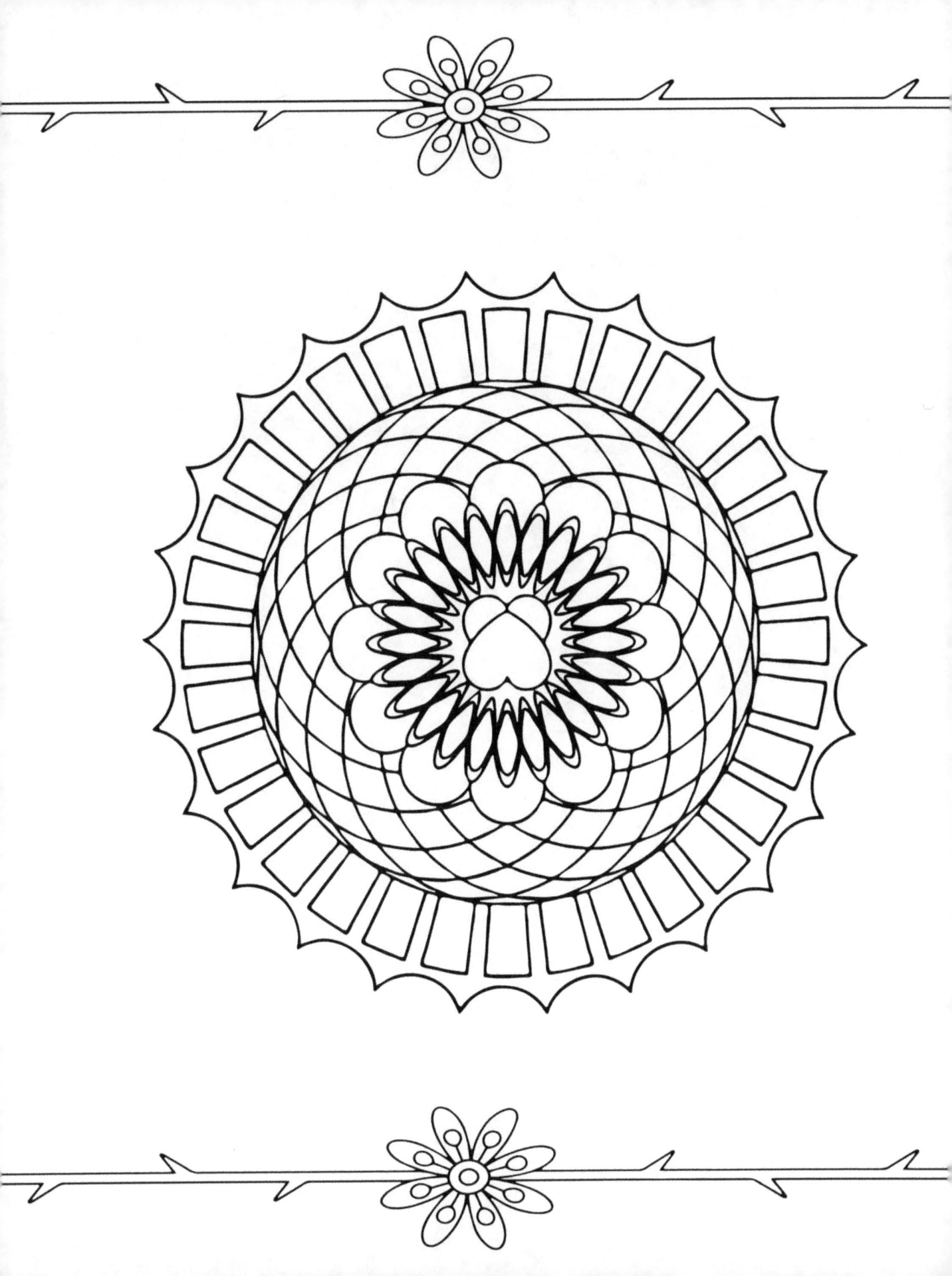

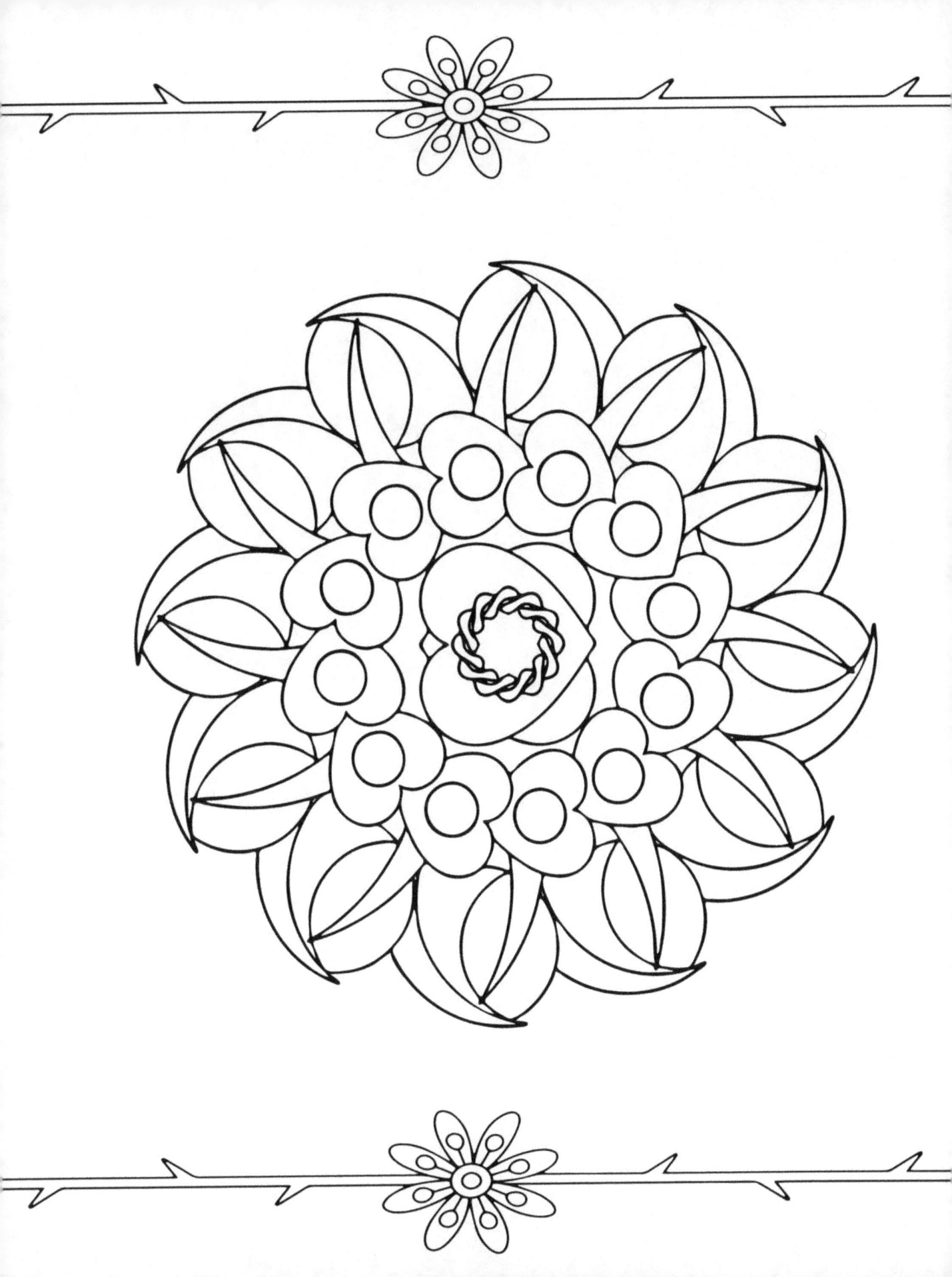

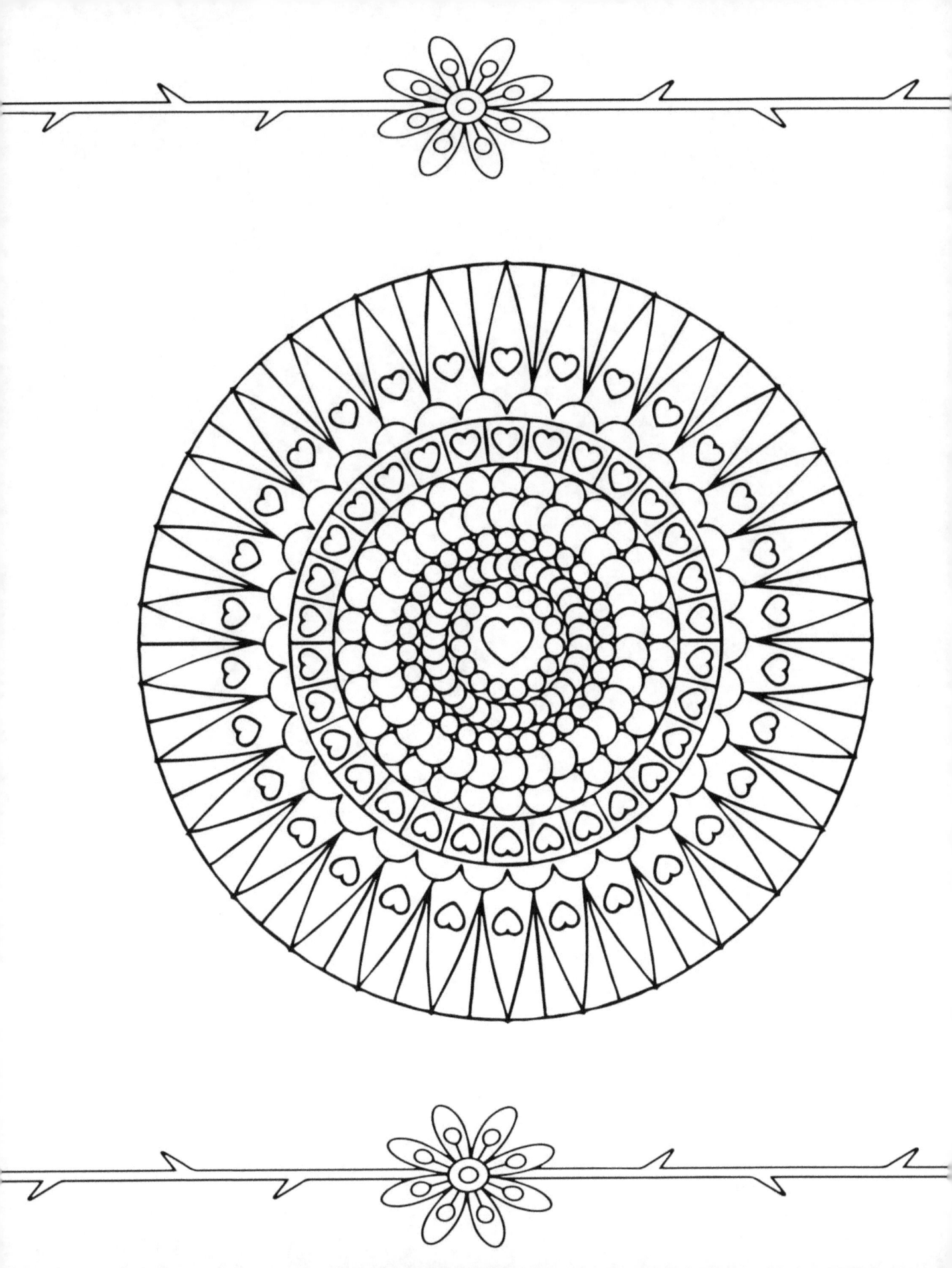

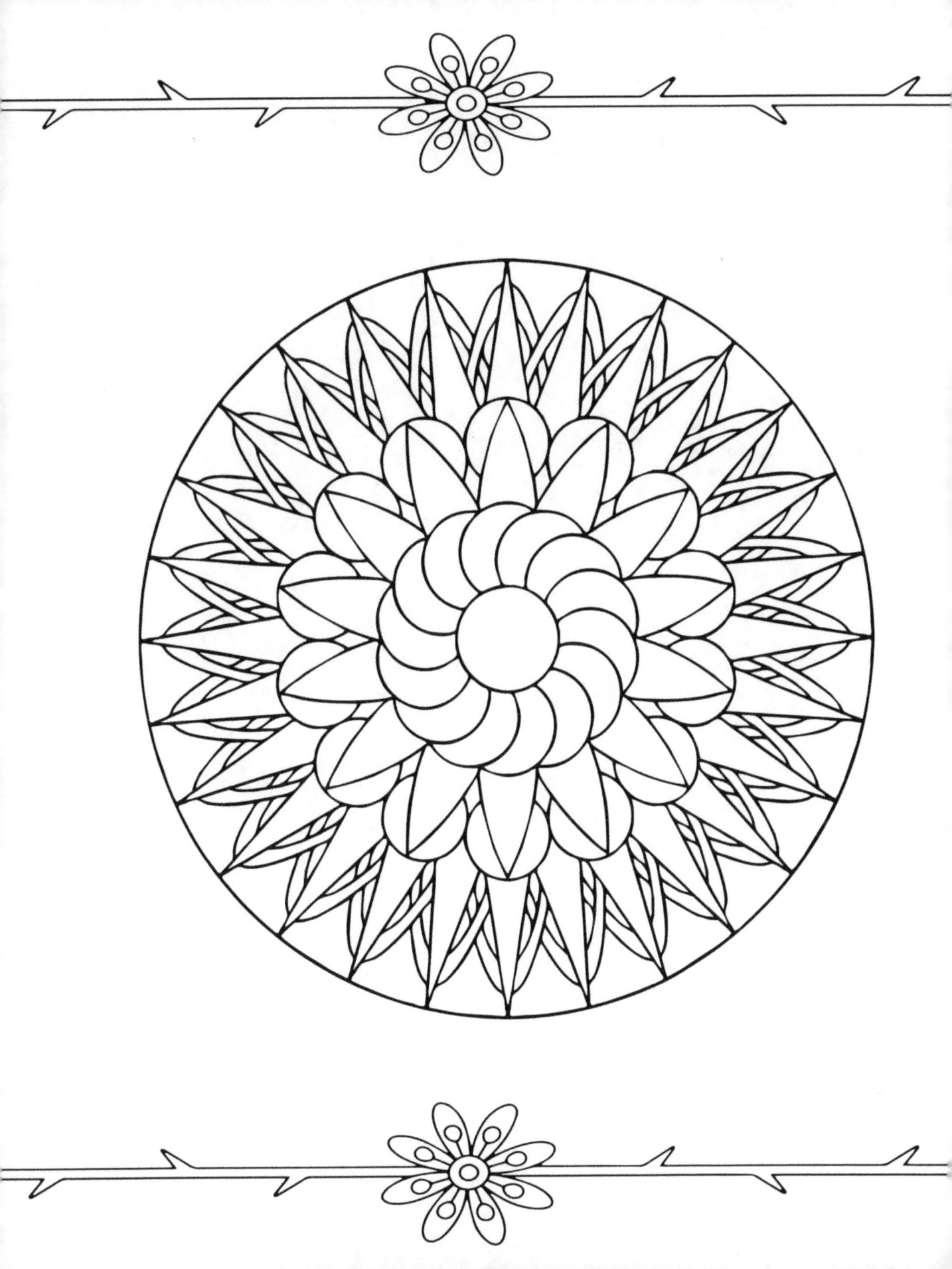

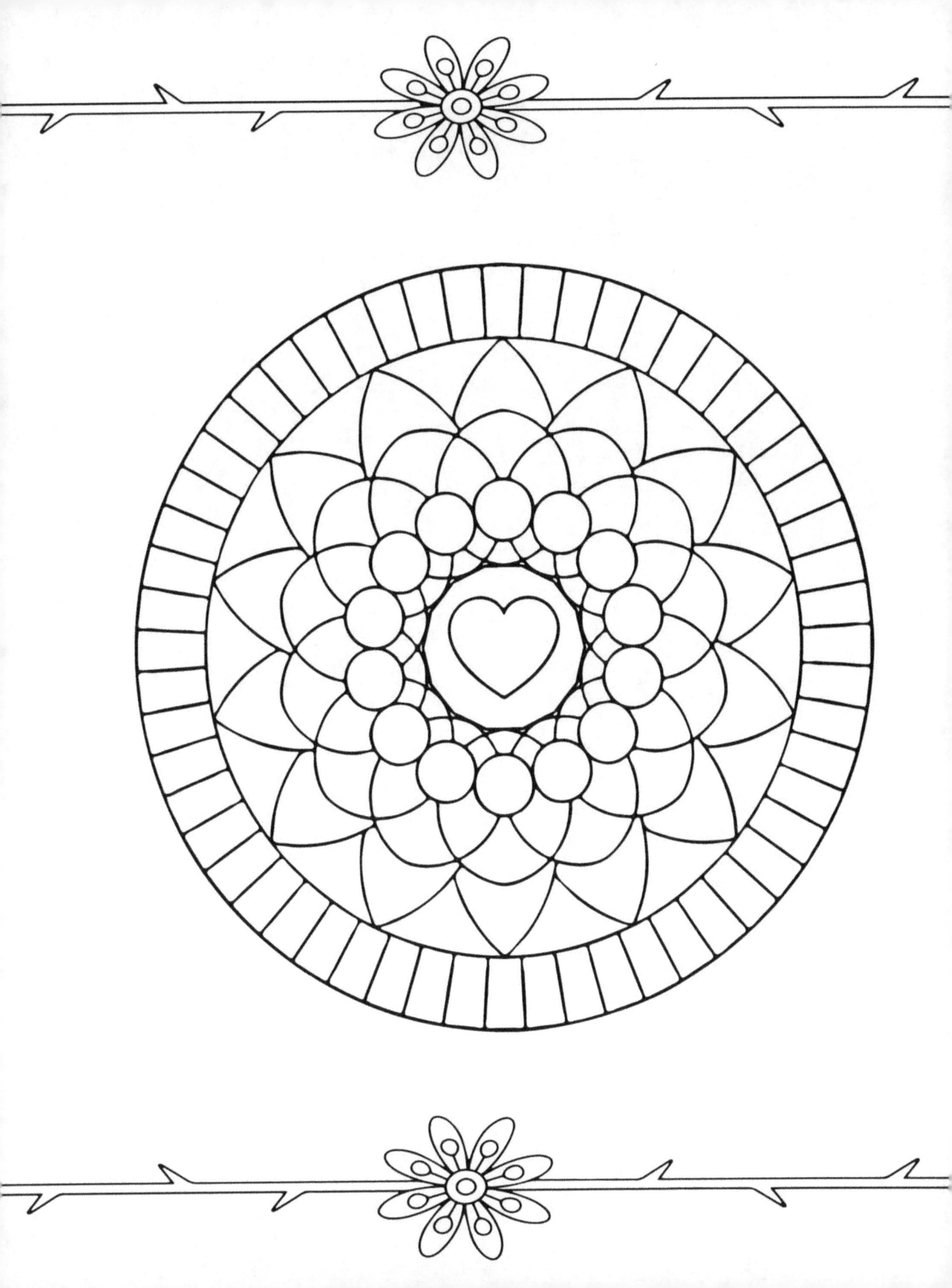

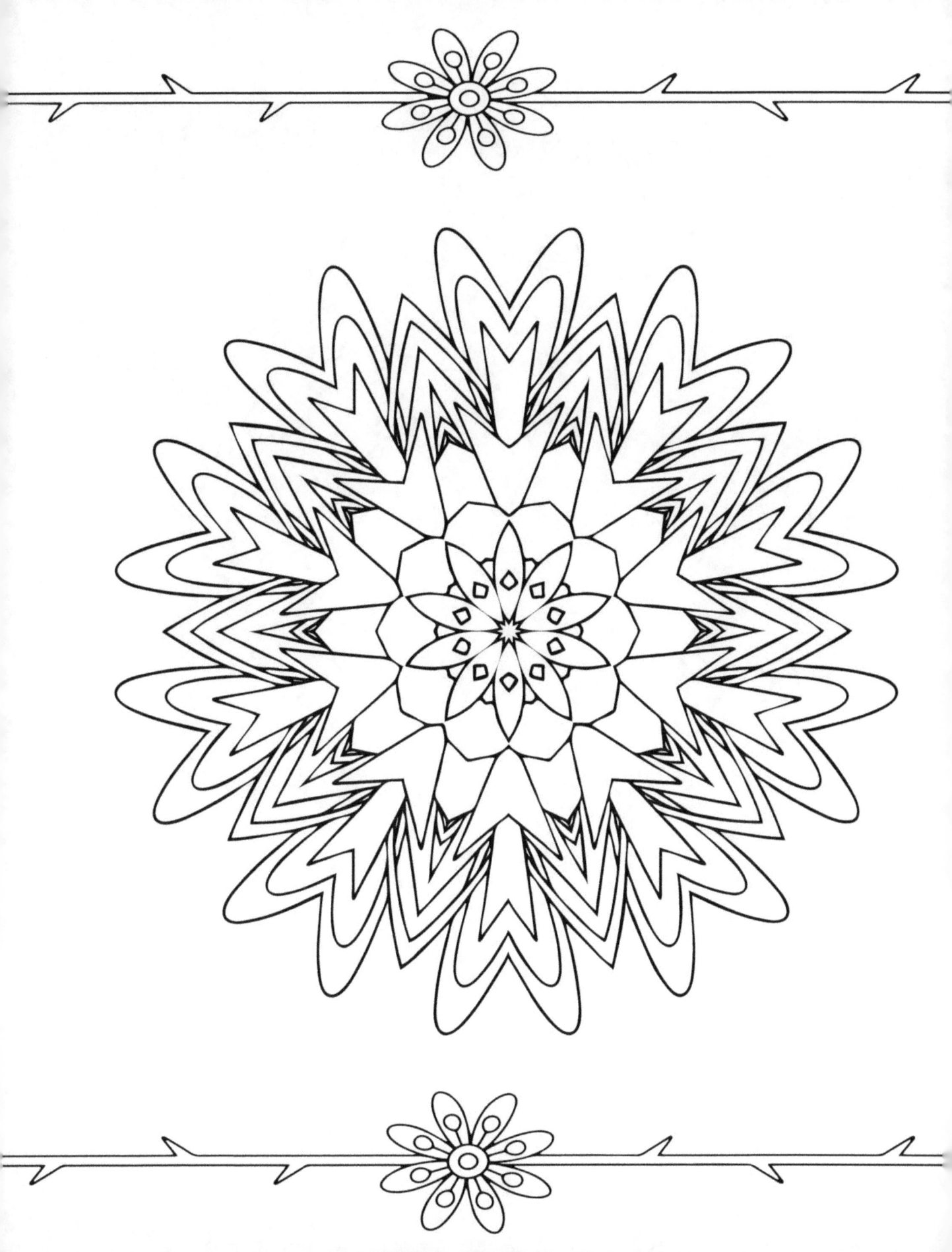

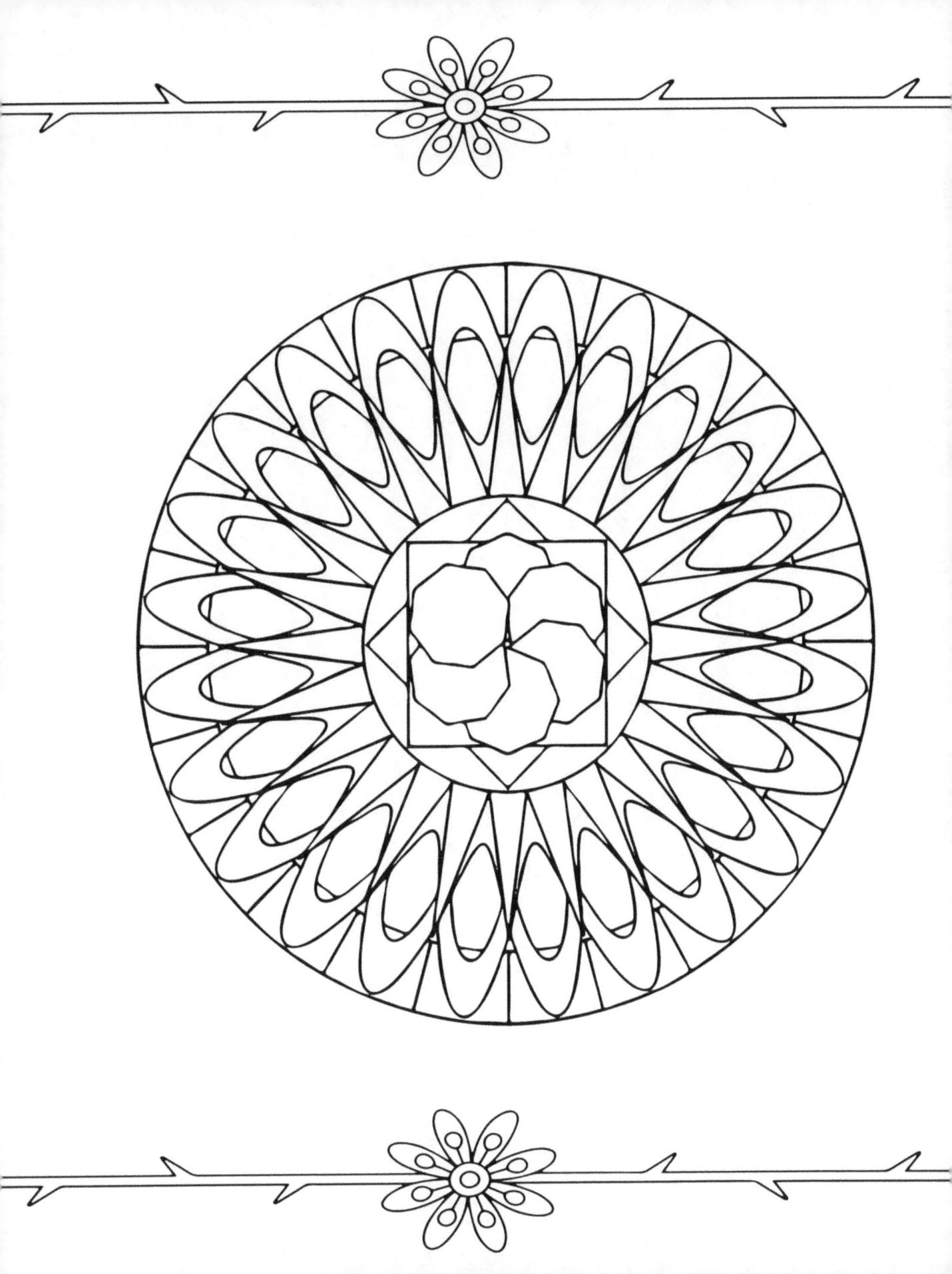

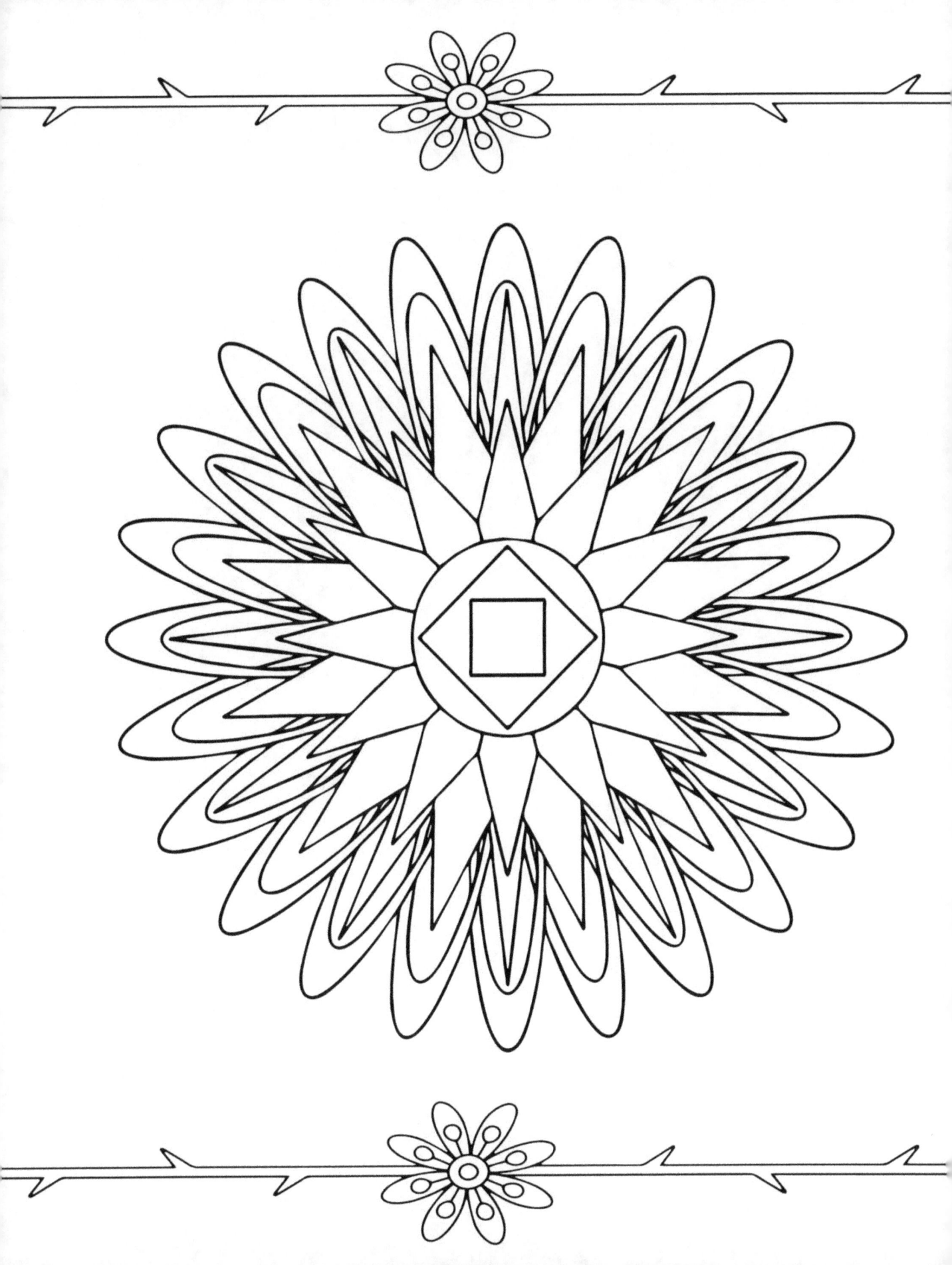

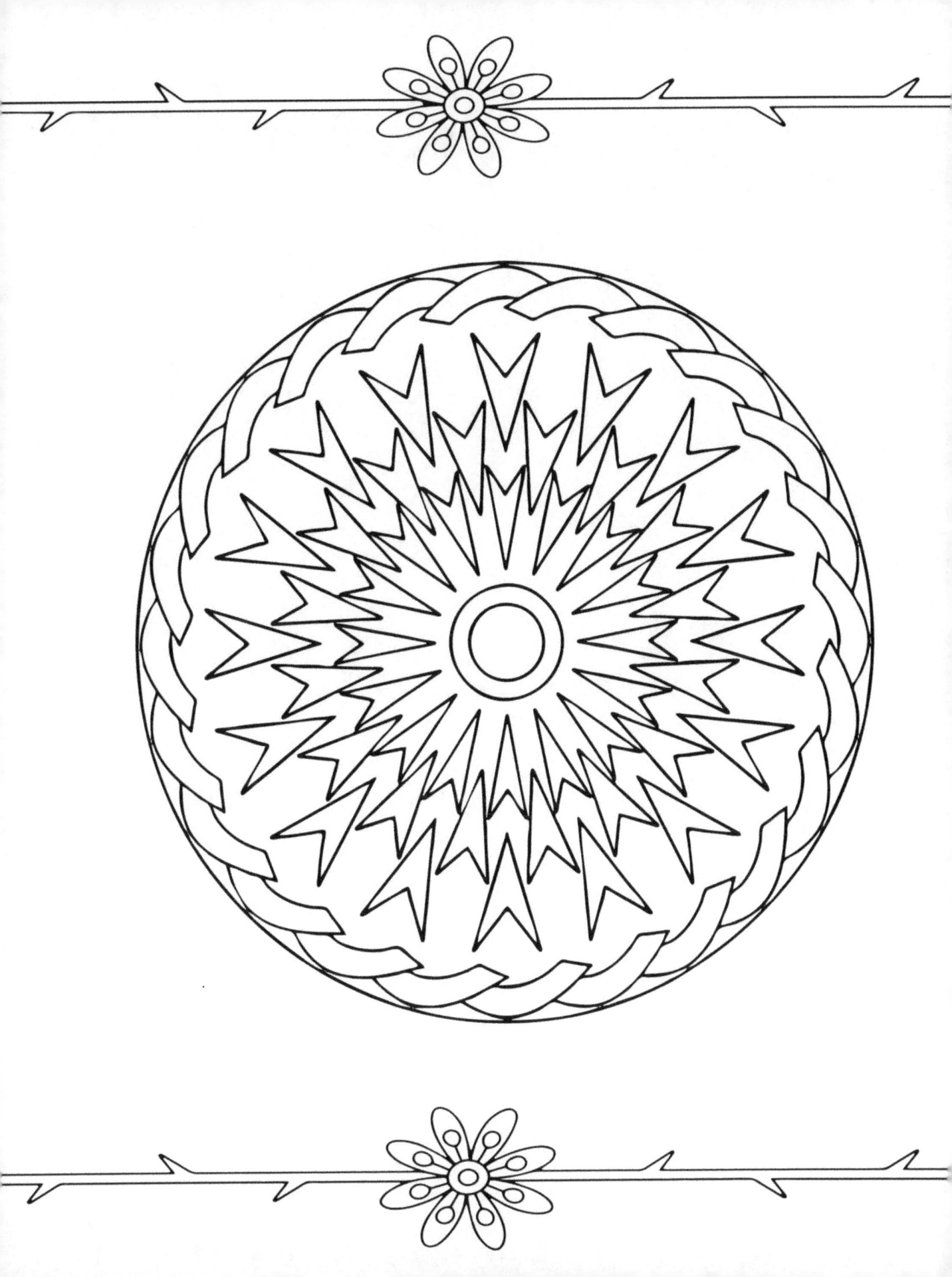

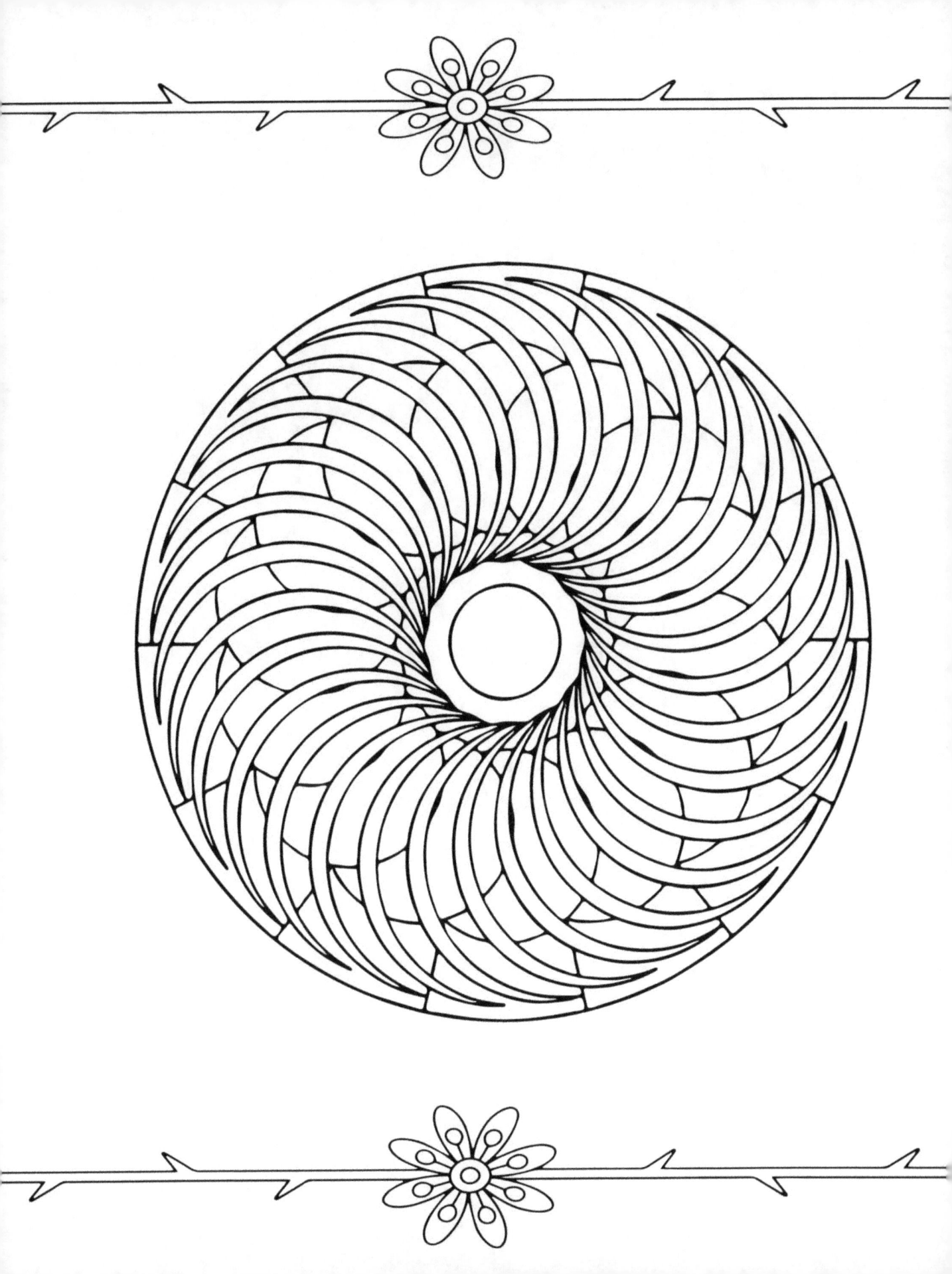

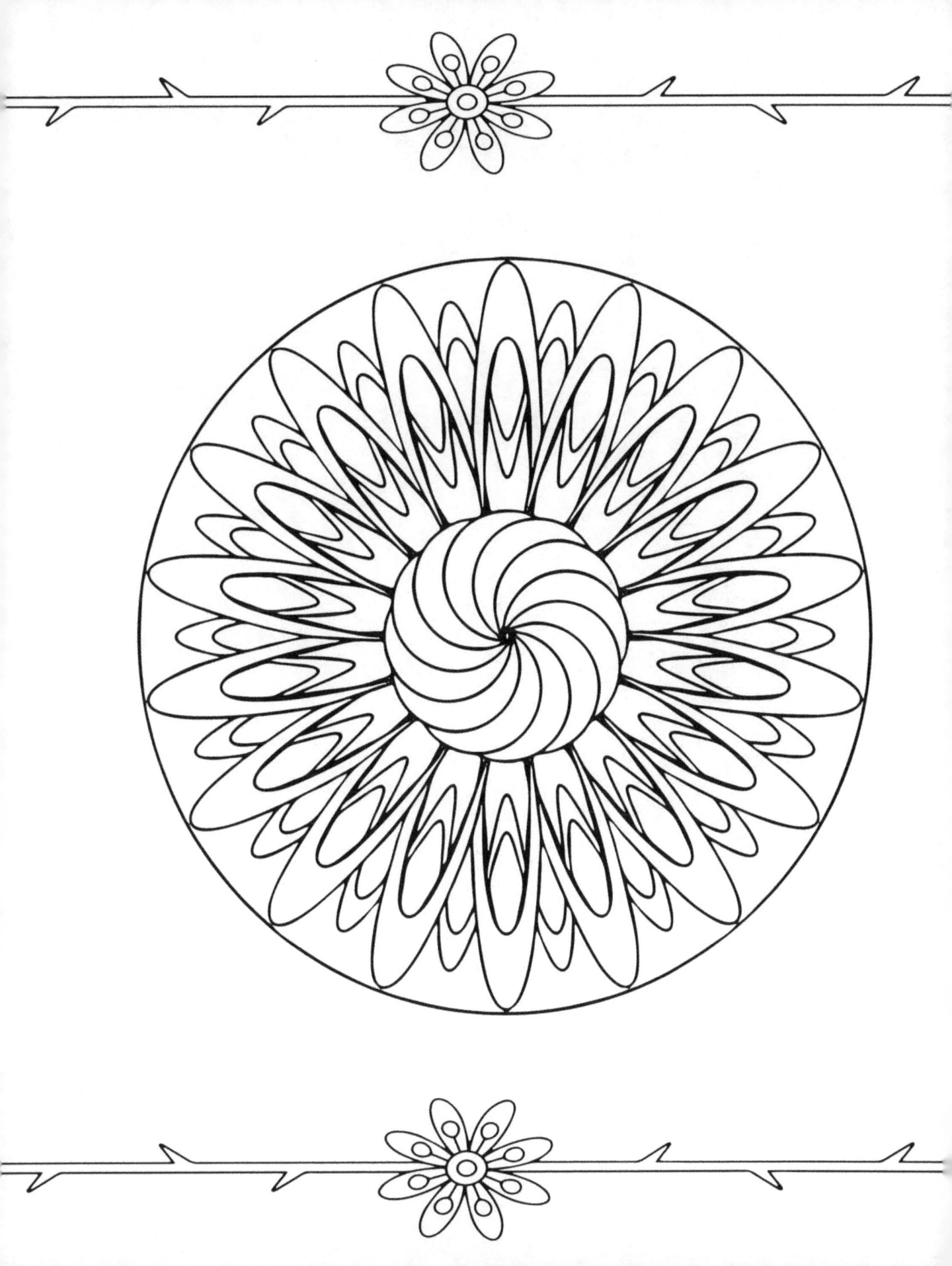

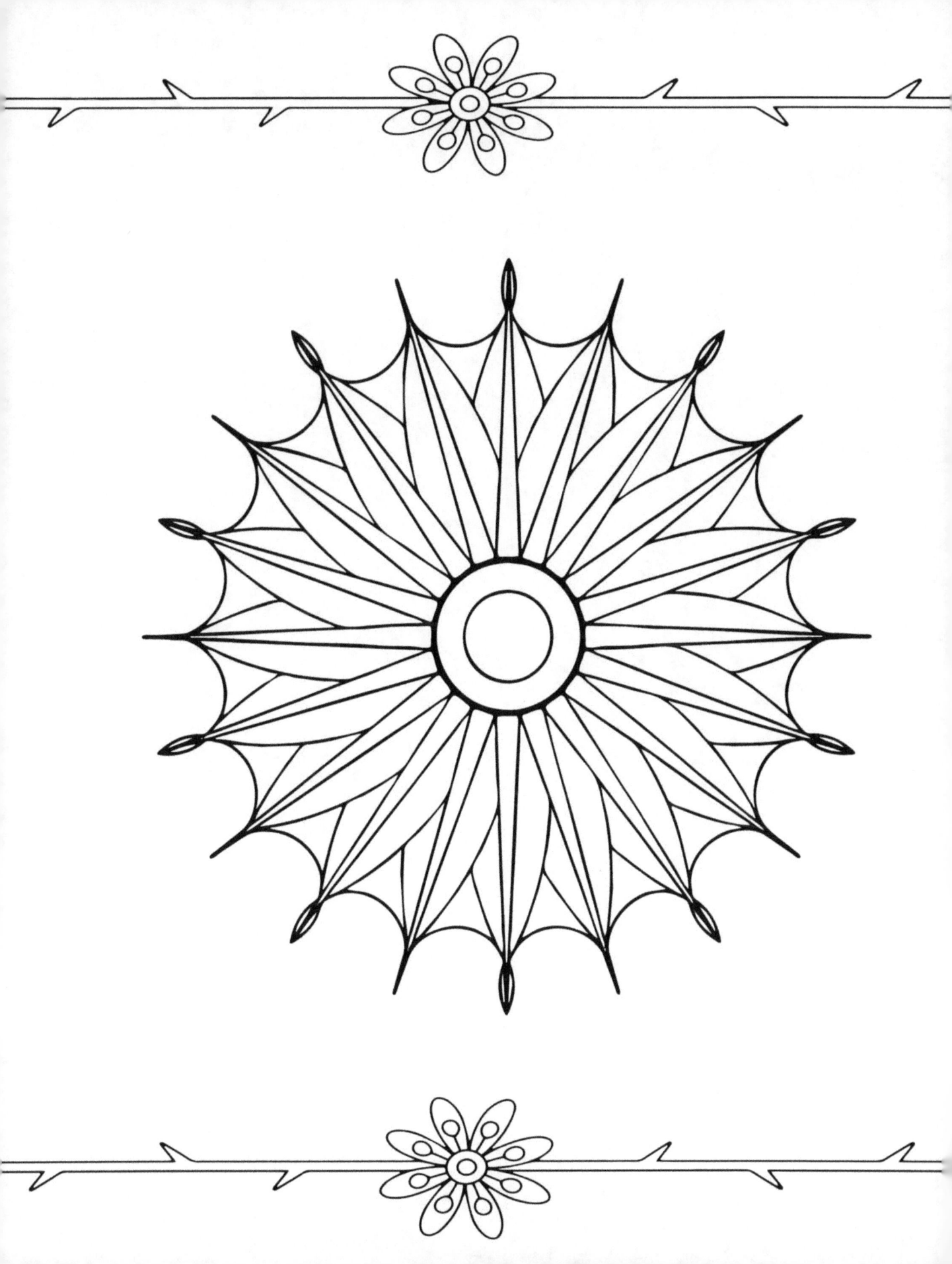

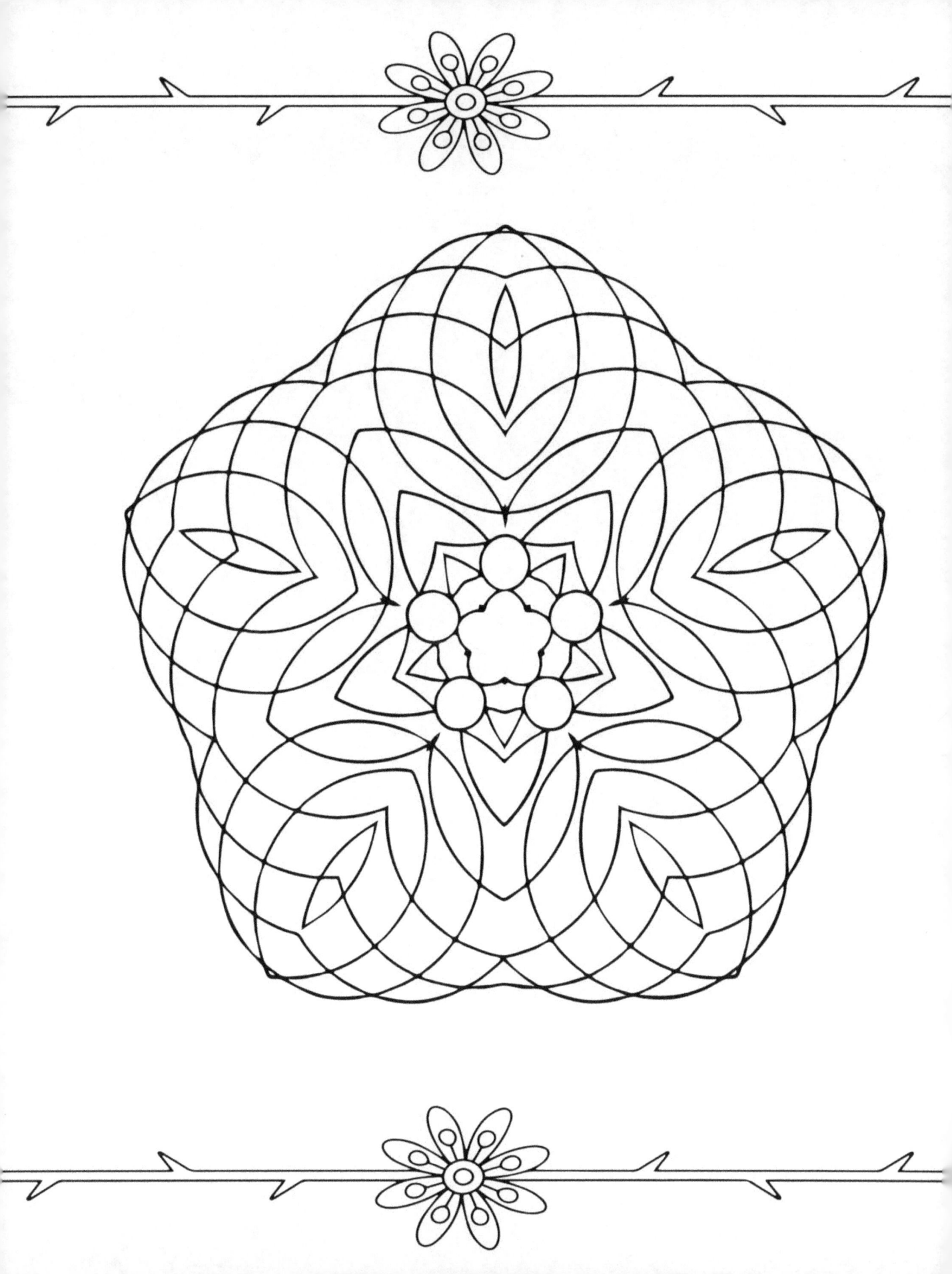

One Last Thing

I hope you have enjoyed colouring the mandalas in this book and that you would be kind enough to consider giving an honest review on Amazon.

Also, look out for the other full sized books in my colouring series where there are many more for you to colour and all available on Amazon.

Please check out my website:

https://charlottegeorgecolouring.com

Best Wishes
Charlotte